I personally congratulate Dr. Brent Price for this incisive and very timely source for personal evangelism. Jesus and Socrates agreed: "Ask questions and listen for the answers." And Jesus answered, "Be ready to give an answer to every man that asketh thee for the hope within you." It's ingenious, it's scriptural, and it works for anyone!

Pat Boone
Internationally Known Entertainer

"Dr. Brent Price has charted an effective soulwinning road map for pointing people to the way of salvation in Jesus Christ. His passion and purity of motive are unquestioned, and his desire to facilitate equipping God's people is a proven pastoral track of his ministry."

Dr. Jack W. Hayford
Pastor Emeritus, The Church On The Way

Dr. Brent Price has created a soulwinning plan that is marvelous in its simplicity and effectiveness. Believers can now quickly learn how to start winning souls in personal evangelism. It is a powerful tool to lead the unsaved to decisions for Jesus Christ in the twenty-first century.

Bishop Charles E. Blake
Pastor
West Angeles Church of God in Christ

"I have been involved in Evangelism for years. Brent Price has written the most exciting and fruitful guide book in personal evangelism for today, a must read for every Believer! It is truly an eye opener on how to win souls for Jesus Christ!"

Chaplain Regina Weller
President, Homeless Task Force

In 2003, I attended a Dr. Brent Price Seminar entitled "How to win souls in personal evangelism." It awakened my view of what personal evangelism actually means and I learned in my opinion to be the most effective salvation gospel presentation used for personal evangelism. I have led over 100 people to Christ by presenting this salvation gospel presentation, including my own Mother. This simple, yet powerful salvation gospel presentation is easy to learn and comfortable to use in daily life.

Grant Huffman, Elder
Calvary Chapel
Corpus Christi, Texas

"Lets cut to the chase. The church of Jesus Christ---at least in America---is not cutting it. We need help. Lots of help. Most churches are not seeing authentic evangelistic growth. Many believers are not effectively sharing the basics of their faith in compelling and magnetic ways. We acknowledge our need for help. Brent Price functions as a "conscience," gently, but persistently, reminging us, "You have something precious to share. So here's how to do it."

Dr. Jim Garlow
CEO/Founder, Well Versed

Dr. Brent Price practices what he preaches! He not only knows how to witness in a unique way, he knows how to teach others to witness and win souls in a powerful and usable way. He is a witnessing man of God and I've even watched him win souls on a golf course! His book and seminar will teach you how to win souls for the Kingdom of God.

Pastor Fred Barber, ret.
Living Branch Foursquare Church
Culver City, Calilfornia

"After 12 years of praying and witnessing, but with little headway, God used Dr. Brent Price's salvation gospel presentation to open the door for me to lead my brother to the Lord as he was dying of Cancer. Pastor Brent's teaching not only helped me recognize the opportunity to "make the ask", but also gave me the practical helps to do so with confidence, love and compassion. I remain eternally grateful.

The Rev. Rob Holman
St. Lukes Anglican Church
Glendale, Calilfornia

WHAT TO SAY
EVANGELISM
The Personal Evangelism Game Changer

Brent Price, D.Min.

WESTBOW
P R E S S®
A DIVISION OF THOMAS NELSON
& ZONDERVAN

WestBow Press books may be ordered through booksellers or by contacting:

WestBow Press
A Division of Thomas Nelson & Zondervan
1663 Liberty Drive
Bloomington, IN 47403
www.westbowpress.com
844-714-3454

ISBN: 978-1-6642-6593-6 (sc)
ISBN: 978-1-6642-6594-3 (e)

Print information available on the last page.

WestBow Press rev. date: 10/02/2023

CONTENTS

A clear biblical message that a Christian does not need to make an unsaved person their new best friend in order to lead them to their decision for Christ.

This explains that Christians can change lives for all eternity with this strategized salvation gospel presentation, but it must be learned to present it.

Christians are to do more than just lead unsaved people to decisions for Christ. Christians should also direct them to their Church or another Church or help them locate a church in their area. A high point encourages leading unsaved family members or friends to Christ on the telephone if they live in another community, state or country.

A fresh view of personal evangelism focusing on win them to Christ first, then invite them to church to then be discipled and equipped. It is easier to win them to Christ, rather than win them to a church visit and see them actually come to Church. A special message to get prepared to win Jews to Christ and be blessed as you do.

DEDICATION

To my wife Beverly, I love you and know that the Lord called us as husband and wife. Thank you for sharing a life journey with me. Thank you for your patience, support and evangelism brainstorming as I worked through this book.

To my daughter Brittney. Your mother and I love and adore you. I am very proud of you and know that the Lord has great things in store for you. At a young age you accepted Jesus as your Savior, learned about life commitments, are a high achiever and I am proud and thrilled to be your father.

To my father, Eldon Andrew Price. Even though you and mother have gone to be with the Lord, you are both constantly in my thoughts and I look forward to being with you both for all eternity.

To my mother, Thelma Rose Price. All of my life I have known that you believed in me. Thank you for a mother's special love that I have cherished every day of my life.

To my two sisters, Sandy Perkins and Cheryl Pany. I deeply love the both of you. Separated, but only by distance, I always look forward to our times together. In your different ways you are both remarkable women and I am proud to be your brother.

ACKNOWLEDGMENTS

To Dr. Jack Hayford, my former Pastor, former President of The Foursquare Church and founder of The Church on the Way in Van Nuys, California. You are a father in the faith to many and along with myself have been a tremendous influence upon countless lives in living out a Spirit led life. I and many others also believe that "Pastor Jack", as he is respectfully and affectionately known, is the preeminent Pastoral theologian of our era.

To John R. Webb Jr., my best friend and brother in Christ. The Lord used you to be a role model for me when I first received Jesus as my Savior. You are also the first person to tell me what scripture to explain to an unsaved person, which turned out to be the first person I led to Christ within two weeks of my own salvation.

To Rev. James L. Obermeyer, a uniquely anointed man of God and great friend, who founded the Beverly Hills Community Church, a Foursquare Church. The Lord used him to call me into pastoral ministry and I will be eternally grateful for his friendship.

To Dr. David Conrad, the Lord used you to develop my interest in the concept of a strategized salvation gospel presentation. You did this at your training on witnessing at First Baptist Van Nuys in Van Nuys, California in preparation to minister at the 1984 Olympics in Los Angeles.

To Rev. Buford Cain, former Pastor of Easthaven Baptist Church in Houston, Texas. It was your advice one Monday morning, "To give God something He can use", that the Lord used to launch me into a life of ministry.

To Rev. Dr. James B. Thompson, former Pastor of Calvary Baptist Church in Beaumont, Texas. The Lord used your powerful messages to teach and prepare me to call on Jesus to be my Savior, which I did on May 2, 1977.

To Michael Ivanoff, thank you for your computer expertise in helping to launch this book.

To the people of Lockhart, Texas. A wonderful little town that I grew up in and to this very day love to visit. It is exciting to be with whomever I can, visit and have some Lockhart barbeque.

To the people of United Methodist Church in Lockhart. A wonderful church filled with precious memories. A special acknowledgment to Geraldine "Gerry" Chesser, my first Sunday School Teacher, that as a young boy, the Lord used her to build into me a love for Jesus Christ.

To the Foursquare Church for giving me the opportunity to Pastor the Beverly Hills Community Church. To the people of The Beverly Hills Community Church whom I will always love, pray for and have cherished memories of for the rest of my life.

To Pastor Steven H. Weller, a great man of God and very special friend who has gone to be with the Lord. He founded Addict's for Christ and The Homeless Task Force. Pastor Steve and his wife Regina Pastored the Venice Foursquare Church and led a very effective ministry in Los Angeles in ministering to the homeless. Steve was a great encourager to go and win souls.

CHAPTER ONE

LEARN WHAT TO SAY TO BE PREPARED TO LEAD UNSAVED PEOPLE TO CHRIST

WHAT TO SAY EVANGELISM has three personal evangelism goals. The First, is to teach and equip men, women and mature teens precisely what to say to win souls in personal evangelism. They can and will learn how to win souls when they learn and understand "what to say and why to say it, who to say it to, when to say it, where to say it and how to say it" in order to lead any unsaved person to accept Jesus Christ as their Savior.

The Second, is identifying the most damaging, but unintentional personal evangelism problem that has negatively impacted the body of Christ for years. This will also include a detailed analysis, which will explain why most Christians have never led a single soul to Christ and are rarely if ever, taught how to win souls in personal evangelism.

The Third, is to identify the biblical personal evangelism role model that the Lord used to teach the body of Christ to be Spirit led in personal evangelism. This Spirit led role model was also used by God to teach the body of Christ what to say in order to be prepared to win or lead any unsaved person to accept Jesus as their Savior. To also identify how the Lord gloriously and very uniquely demonstrated His affirmation of him as the personal evangelism role model.

LEARN WHAT TO SAY TO KNOW WHAT
TO SAY IN PERSONAL EVANGELISM

To know what to say in personal evangelism can now be easily learned. To know what to say, learn the one of a kind, "biblically strategized salvation gospel presentation." It is a unique salvation gospel presentation, that I first developed when I helped lead an evangelistic outreach to the 1984 Olympics in Los Angeles, California. The start of this salvation gospel presentation is precisely what to say, that will instantly create a desire in unsaved family members, friends or strangers to want to hear the salvation gospel. Upon hearing it, they will want to immediately pray and will pray to accept Jesus Christ as their Savior.

After you learn it, you will know what to say and will be prepared as the Holy Spirt or an Angel of the Lord leads or prompts you to begin this salvation gospel presentation. You may be in the midst of witnessing or simply having a general conversation with any unsaved person. Then suddenly, when the time is right, the Holy Spirit or an Angel of the Lord will prompt or impress you to shift or transition out of the current conversation and begin presenting the salvation gospel presentation. Only the Lord knows the right time to present the salvation gospel presentation. He will always be with you. He will lead you, which can also mean to prompt or impress you. He will let you know, no matter what kind of conversation you are having, when it is time to politely phase it out. To then gently begin presenting the salvation gospel presentation.

THE HOLY SPIRIT OR AN ANGEL KNOWS WHO
IS READY TO HEAR AND RECEIVE CHRIST

A situation could arise when the Lord knows that someone that you do not know is ready to hear the salvation gospel presentation. What to say to any unsaved person in order to lead them to Christ, no matter if you know them or not, is completely prepared for you with the biblically strategized salvation gospel presentation. Whether you know an unsaved person or not does not matter. The Holy Spirit or an Angel knows them, their life history and why they are now ready to hear and receive the salvation gospel. You do not need to know their history or why they are now ready to hear and receive the salvation gospel. Your role is to be prepared to present the salvation gospel presentation to them. When any unsaved person hears this prepared salvation gospel presentation, 95% to 100% of the time they completely understand the need to, will want to and will immediately pray to accept Jesus Christ as their Savior.

WHAT TO SAY IS PREPARED FOR YOU
TO LEARN AND TO PRESENT

The biblically strategized salvation gospel presentation is designed to clearly explain biblical language that any unsaved person will easily understand and follow, that will lead them to their decision to accept Jesus Christ as their Savior.

This easily understood salvation gospel presentation will then gently conclude with an already prepared and brief salvation prayer. A prepared, word for word brief prayer, for you to tell any unsaved person what they need to pray to accept Jesus Christ as their Savior. After hearing this salvation gospel presentation, unsaved people are completely evangelized and are ready to and want to accept Jesus Christ as their Savior. They are willing to pray to accept Jesus as their Savior and they will pray, as you gently tell them from the prepared prayer what to pray to accept Jesus Christ as their Savior.

BASIC PERSONAL EVANGELISM WORDS OR PHRASES

In personal evangelism words or phrases such as "win or win souls, reap or reap a harvest, led or lead to Christ" all mean the same thing. They mean that whatever the circumstances happen to be, when a man, woman or mature teen presents the biblically strategized salvation gospel presentation to an unsaved person, the unsaved person will respond by immediately praying to accept Jesus as their Savior.

Additional words or phrases such as "the Lord led, is leading, led, lead, impress, prompt or letting you know" all refer to or identify for the purposes of this teaching, that you are being led by the Holy Spirit or an Angel of the Lord. These are for you to realize that you are being "led by the Spirit" Rom 8:14 "For as many as are led by the Spirit of God, these are the sons of God." The Holy Spirit or an Angel of the Lord is encouraging you to present this unique salvation gospel presentation to lead an unsaved person to their decision to accept Jesus Christ as their Savior.

TO BE PREPARED FOR PERSONAL EVANGELISM
YOU MUST KNOW WHAT TO SAY

When I first began developing the biblically strategized salvation gospel presentation, I did not realize that what the Lord was leading me to say to unsaved people in order to lead them to their decision for Christ, was what the bible actually models and teaches to say to unsaved people. This salvation gospel presentation is extremely successful, because it duplicates the same "personal evangelism subject matter and strategized salvation gospel presentation model" that is in the bible. For your own personal evangelism, you are about to learn what to say and will be prepared to introduce, present and conclude the salvation gospel with salvation results.

To clarify, an immediate salvation result means that at the end of hearing the biblically strategized salvation gospel presentation, any unsaved person will want to pray and will pray to accept Jesus Christ as their Savior. That is the predictable and consistent personal evangelism result with this biblical salvation gospel presentation, which is why this book is entitled WHAT TO SAY EVANGELISM.

SAY AND DO WHAT THE BIBLE TEACHES TO SAY AND DO

You will discover as you continue through this teaching, "what to say and do" are in the bible as a "role model example", which is broadly explained and detailed, along with the salvation gospel presentation. The detailed explanation is for men, women and mature teens to learn and deeply understand "what to say and why to say it, who to say it to, when to say it, where to say it and how to say it" in order to lead unsaved people to their immediate decisions to accept Jesus Christ as their own Savior.

BE PREPARED TO WIN SOULS BIBLICALLY

Moving forward, you will find many references to the phrase, "biblically strategized salvation gospel presentation." They are there as an encouraging reminder, that this salvation gospel presentation is the biblical answer to all of the challenging questions and concerns around the issue of "how to win souls, how to lead or win unsaved people to immediate decisions for Christ in personal evangelism." Together, our mission and goal must always be to lead or win unsaved people to immediate decisions for Christ. Their eternal lives depend upon it. To then encourage and direct them as new Christians, to a church, home group, cell group or a bible study for discipleship. With so many references about decisions, a timely question is how long does it take for people to make a decision? In particular, how long does it take for an unsaved person to make a decision to accept Jesus Christ as their Savior? The answer is that all people gather information in order to make a decision about any life issue.

People gather information and sometimes it takes time to get all the information they want in order to make their decision. When they get the information that they think they need to make their decision, their moment of decision, is immediate, as fast as the "blink of an eye." This is exactly what will take place with unsaved people when men, women and mature teens learn and begin to present the biblically strategized salvation gospel presentation to unsaved people. Immediate decisions for Christ take place because this brief, but powerful salvation gospel presentation answers the most critical concern and fear that all unsaved people have in life, which is what happens to them at their own coming death. When unsaved people hear the biblical answer for themselves through this salvation gospel presentation, they immediately, "in the blink of an eye," make their decision to accept Jesus Christ as their Savior.

WHY THE BIBLICALLY STRATEGIZED
SALVATION GOSPEL PRESENTATION

The creation and development of the biblically strategized salvation gospel presentation has one purpose and goal. That ultimate purpose and goal is to train and equip men, women and mature teens to be prepared under any circumstances, to know what to say to introduce, present and conclude the salvation gospel of Jesus Christ with an immediate salvation result. When Christian's present this biblically strategized salvation gospel presentation, they can do so assured that around 95% to 100% of every unsaved person they present it to will immediately accept Jesus Christ as their Savior.

This will happen for men, women and mature teens, because this complete teaching and the biblically strategized salvation gospel presentation will totally equip and prepare them to actually lead or win unsaved people to immediate decisions for Christ. They can and will do this, because they will be prepared the same way that the bible teaches and models exactly how to lead or win unsaved people to immediate decisions for Christ in personal evangelism. Leading or winning unsaved people to accept and receive Jesus Christ as Savior in personal evangelism is not hard. It is in fact, an easy thing for men, women and mature teens to do, but only after they learn "what to say and why to say it, who to say it to, when to say it, where to say it and how to say it." In any life endeavor the key to success is to always trust the Lord and be prepared to accomplish the task at hand.

"Leading unsaved people to immediate decisions for Christ with the biblically strategized salvation gospel presentation is not rocket science. It is more important than rocket science, but it is not rocket science."

Brent Price

PERSONAL EVANGELISM PROBLEMS AND THE BIBLICAL SOLUTION

You are also going to learn in great detail why around 95% of all Christians have never led a single unsaved person to accept and receive Jesus as their Savior. The 95% number has been around for decades and most in ministry leadership agree that it is fairly accurate. Whatever the actual number is and only the Lord knows what it is, these numbers represent untold millions of Christians who have never led or won a single unsaved person to Christ. The following observations and conclusions are from over 35 years of pursuing answers about the "problems and reason why" most Christians do not witness or have never led a single unsaved person to Christ. The biblically strategized salvation gospel presentation is the answer and solution to every personal evangelism problem and challenge.

IN PERSONAL EVANGELISM MOST HAVE THE SAME PROBLEMS

Over many years, I have spoken with a large number of men and women from different denominations about the broad variety of personal evangelism situations and problems that they encountered. I did this to not only teach them how to lead or win unsaved people to Christ, but to discover their views, fears and concerns about actually participating in personal evangelism. I discovered that their many fears and concerns were all similar, individualized and quite frustrating to them. I discovered that the "core or deep" personal evangelism problem is almost exclusively from not knowing what to say in order to introduce, present and conclude the salvation gospel with an immediate salvation result. In personal evangelism, leading or winning any unsaved person to an immediate decision to accept Jesus as their Savior can take place anywhere and anytime. The thought of any unsaved person dying and being eternally separated from God in hell is terrifying and horrible. Men, women and mature teens can now learn how to lead or win any unsaved person to Jesus Christ as their Savior and be used of the Lord as He saves them from going to hell.

THE BIBLICALLY STRATEGIZED SALVATION GOSPEL PRESENTATION GIVES "GO WITNESS" A BALANCE IN PERSONAL EVANGELISM

The biblically strategized salvation gospel presentation is the personal evangelism game changer, because it gives men, women and mature teens a much needed balance in their personal evangelism. Christians are encouraged to "Go witness, share their faith, share the Lord, share their personal testimony, build relationships to effectively witness or invite unsaved people to church." The problem is that these traditional personal evangelism encouragements are not balanced, because they are basic sowing processes and have no direction, structure, strategy or goal or training on what to say to unsaved people in order to lead or reap them to a decision for Christ.

When Christians are not taught what to say to unsaved people and with no direction or goal to win a soul, they are unintentionally only prepared to timidly or generally witness. This is the problem that has created a massive intimidating reluctance to witness throughout the body of Christ. The result of this problem is that when many Christians do witness, it is generalized, with few decisions for Christ. The balance is when Christians are told to go witness, but now with the biblically strategized salvation gospel presentation they will know precisely what to say. What to say in order to transition out of general or vague witnessing and actually lead any unsaved person to an immediate decision for Christ.

General or vague witnessing is good, fine and normal, but needs to be balanced with the biblically strategized salvation gospel presentation. To then know precisely what to say to introduce, present and conclude this salvation gospel presentation with a salvation result almost 100% of the time.

THE UNSAVED SHOULD BE LED NOT TOLD WHAT TO DO NOT LECTURED CONDEMNED OR CRITICIZED

Most, if not all unsaved people who have been witnessed to have heard a vast array of witnessing reasons and justifications from Christians as to why they need to accept Jesus as their Savior. Many Christians have tried to "talk them into, tell them they need to, explain, pronounce or rationalize the need to" accept Christ. At times, some Christians unfortunately end up sounding like they were criticizing or giving a condemning put down type lecture. These things can easily happen and do happen, because far too many Christians are not equipped and prepared to biblically and understandably explain the need to accept Jesus Christ as their Savior. These are just some of the reasons why, from negative personal evangelism experiences, many unsaved people do not accept Him as their Savior and end up getting turned off to Jesus Christ, Christians or church in general.

Unsaved people do not want to be "told what to do or lectured about what to do, put down and certainly not condemned", but are willing to "be led" into what to do. The biblically strategized salvation gospel presentation leads the unsaved to Christ and will eliminate lecturing or condemning style witnessing and give vague or general witnessing a new and fresh direction with balance. It is like nothing an unsaved person has ever heard before and they are unprepared for it.

Upon hearing this salvation gospel presentation, their defenses and preconceived notions are eliminated, because the word of God in this prepared salvation gospel presentation powerfully impacts and draws them to want Jesus as their Savior. Even if unsaved people have been witnessed to many times before, with this salvation gospel presentation, they are still easily led and they will immediately accept Jesus as their Savior.

WITNESSING NEEDS BALANCE TO INTRODUCE, PRESENT AND CONCLUDE THE SALVATION GOSPEL WITH IMMEDIATE SALVATION RESULTS

Almost every Christian who is willing to witness or considers witnessing is challenged with the classic question of "what do I say to unsaved people?" The personal evangelism game changer is that Christians can now be balanced in their personal evangelism by learning the biblically strategized salvation gospel presentation. The balance that comes with this salvation gospel presentation is that men, women and mature teens will now be prepared to change, transition or shift from general witnessing or a general conversation about anything and know precisely what to say in order to introduce, present and conclude the salvation gospel with immediate salvation results. Ultimately, every Christian needs to know "what to say and why to say it, who to say it to, when to say it, where to say it and how to say it" in order to lead unsaved family members, friends or an occasional stranger to their immediate decision for Christ.

THE BIBLICALLY STRATEGIZED SALVATION GOSPEL PRESENTATION IS NOT TO GENERALLY WITNESS

The goal of the biblically strategized salvation gospel presentation is not to generally witness. It is for men, women and mature teens to be prepared with the ability to change, transition or shift into the biblically strategized salvation gospel presentation and bring any conversation with an unsaved person to a conclusion with an immediate salvation result. All interactions between Christians and unsaved people can have a life of its own. The biblically strategized salvation gospel presentation gives Christians a tremendous amount of assurance and confidence. This confidence is from knowing, that no matter who the unsaved person is or what is being discussed, that Christians will always know they can stop general witnessing or a general conversation and start presenting the salvation gospel.

FIRST PREPARE UNSAVED PEOPLE TO WANT TO HEAR THE SALVATION GOSPEL OF JESUS CHRIST

The gospel means the "good news" about Jesus Christ and there is endless good news about Him. The biblically strategized salvation gospel presentation that you will learn, focuses on the "salvation good news" about Him. The good and glorious good news about Jesus Christ is that salvation is in Him and only in Him. You are about to learn how to uniquely present this good news in a way that unsaved people will hear, understand and want to immediately receive His salvation good news for themselves.

Evangelism is spreading, carrying or taking and presenting the good news to the unsaved world. Unfortunately, in personal evangelism, spreading, carrying or taking and presenting the good news through general witnessing, faith sharing or in a personal testimony context, almost never concludes with an immediate salvation result. This salvation gospel presentation completely solves this problem.

An extremely important part of the biblically strategized salvation gospel presentation is the beginning when it creates an immediate desire in any unsaved person to want to hear the salvation gospel of Jesus Christ. A lot of general witnessing is telling or talking about Jesus, His work on the cross or what He can accomplish in an unsaved person's life before they are interested in hearing about it. General witnessing can then sound like or can come across as lecturing, talking down to or condemning an unsaved person.

The Holy Spirt or an Angel will lead you or prompt you to start the salvation gospel presentation, because He knows when the unsaved person is ready and willing for whatever reason, to hear the salvation gospel of Jesus Christ and accept Him as their Savior.

THE BIBLICALLY STRATEGIZED SALVATION GOSPEL PRESENTATION EXPLAINS THE NEED TO BE SAVED

It is the unique introduction of the biblically strategized salvation gospel presentation that creates a teachable moment in unsaved people. The salvation gospel presentation will clearly and understandably explain to any unsaved person, why they need to immediately accept Jesus as their Savior. At the end of the biblically strategized salvation gospel presentation there is a designed conclusion, that is simple to present, in order to lead unsaved people through a short prayer as they respond and immediately accept Jesus as their Savior. The biblically strategized salvation gospel presentation is uncomplicated to learn and easy to present to any unsaved person. At the end of the salvation gospel presentation there is a designed conclusion that is low key and gentle. This conclusion, also includes what to say to lead unsaved people in a simple prayer for them to immediately accept Jesus as their Savior. They heard the salvation gospel in an understandable way, made their decision to accept Jesus as the Savior and will want to immediately pray to accept Him as their Savior.

TREMENDOUS RESULTS FOR WHAT CHRISTIANS WANT TO KNOW

The result of creating a teachable moment by strategically preparing unsaved people to instantly want to hear this uniquely strategized salvation gospel presentation is huge. The result is that 95% to 100% of the unsaved people that hear it, pray to accept Jesus as their Savior. Over the years every single person I have spoken with who has a concern for unsaved family members, unsaved friends and even an occasional stranger, basically all want to know the same thing. They all want to know specifically or some variation of "What do I say, when do I say it or what should I not say" to an unsaved person to lead or win them to a decision for Christ. You are going to learn word for word, everything you need to say with this salvation gospel presentation in order to immediately lead or win any unsaved person to Christ. To accept and receive Jesus as their Savior means that unsaved people accept that Jesus is the Savior and they will also receive Him as their own Savior.

WHAT THE BIBLICALLY STRATEGIZED SALVATION GOSPEL PRESENTATION IS AND IS NOT

The biblically strategized salvation gospel presentation is not to learn what to say word for word in order to "generally witness, share personal testimony or have general conversations." It is to learn precisely what to say when men, women and mature teens feel or sense that the Holy Spirit has led them to start the biblically strategized salvation gospel presentation. You may sense or feel an urge, you may sense or feel prompted, you may sense or feel now is the time to act. This is the realization that this is the time to change, transition or shift from "general witnessing, sharing personal testimony or a general conversation."

You will quickly discover that it is easy to comfortably introduce, present and conclude the salvation gospel of Jesus Christ with an immediate salvation result. Once you learn the biblically strategized salvation gospel presentation, this is how you may sense or feel being led by the Holy Spirit or an Angel. This is why it is a Spirit led salvation gospel presentation.

WHERE I DEVELOPED THE BIBLICALLY STRATEGIZED SALVATION GOSPEL PRESENTATION

I first developed the highly successful biblically strategized salvation gospel presentation when I helped lead an evangelistic outreach to the 1984 Olympics in Los Angeles, California. This was when I was the Minister to Singles at a large Southern Baptist Church in the Los Angeles area. A ministry from Texas, named Lay Witness for Christ had a ministry focused on athletes at the collegiate and professional level. During the 1984 Olympics they were using the facilities at our church as a headquarters location for their outreach to the Olympic Village area. My role was to encourage single adults to participate in a training on how to witness and then go to the Olympic Village to reach out to the people that were there to see the Olympic Games.

HE PROMOTED WINNING SOULS AS THE GOAL

We went to the witnessing training, led by Dr. David Conrad from a non-denominational church. His training was excellent and focused on what he told unsaved people in his office. He shared or presented around fifteen scriptures to unsaved people at his church. I felt this was to extensive for what we were going to do at the Olympic Village. What got my attention was that the gospel message he presented to unsaved people had a beginning, a middle and a conclusion. This was the first time I had encountered a personal evangelism training that encouraged leading an unsaved person to an immediate decision to accept Jesus as their Savior. After the training I asked him if we could meet to discuss witnessing ideas and we did. Up until this time I may have led five or six unsaved people to decisions for Christ and so I was very interested in learning more. The plan was to go to the Olympic Village on the first Saturday of the Olympics. We all had white T-shirts with LAY WITNESS FOR CHRIST emblazoned on the front. We had our bibles and flyers to hand out letting people know that the Olympian Carl Lewis was going to speak at our church, the next Wednesday night.

Most of the people that went were from the Singles Ministry and we rode in a church school bus and were scheduled to be at the Olympic Village for three hours. People by the thousands, from all over the world were at the Olympics and we went all over the village area. After the three hour outreach we re-assembled and everyone was excited and shared that they all "witnessed" to someone. I shared that I led 9 unsaved people to immediate decisions for Christ. The Lord led me on what to say to unsaved people and the Olympic outreach on that day was how I began developing what I eventually named the "biblically strategized salvation gospel presentation."

OLYMPIANS WON MEDALS I WON SOULS

The next day was Sunday and that night the Lord led me to go back on my own to the Olympic Village to win souls. I had tickets to most of the track events and so I went to the games wearing my t-shirt, with my bible and flyer and in the Olympic Village area over the next three days led 107 unsaved people from all over the world to immediate decisions for Christ. I had follow-up cards on those I led to Christ, which I filled out and turned them all in to the Southern Baptist Venue at the Olympic Village. I still pray for those I led to Christ at the Olympics. I led men, women, boys and girls of all ages and every race and background. This was an incredible experience for me, but it took a lot of time for me to understand and figure out what I just did and what the Lord did in me. It has been a long, but exciting Journey that has culminated in this teaching, WHAT TO SAY EVANGELISM. It was at the 1984 Olympics evangelism outreach that I first developed this salvation gospel presentation and over the years refined it into the biblically strategized salvation gospel presentation that I offer you now.

I LED MY OWN FATHER AND MOTHER IN-LAW TO CHRIST

Over the years I have taught and trained untold numbers of men, women and mature teens, just like you, how to lead unsaved people to immediately accept Jesus as Savior. I personally to this day and will for the rest of my life, still lead unsaved people to Christ with precisely the same biblically strategized salvation gospel presentation that you are about to learn. I have led countless numbers of men, women, boys and girls to Christ, including my own Father and Mother in-law. I have led men, women, boys, girls of all ages, homeless people, teachers, a JPL astrophysicist, plumbers, salesmen, gamblers, atheists, Buddhists, Muslims, business owners, attorneys, a judge, a pro basketball player and people from practically every background imaginable, to their immediate decisions for Christ. I led a well known actor to Christ and nine years later, he won the Academy Award for Best Actor. I led this movie star and all the others to Christ with exactly the same biblically strategized salvation gospel presentation that you are going to learn.

ONE IMPORTANT THING MAKES THEM ALL THE SAME

All of these men, women, boys and girls were from every gender, race, educational, economic, professional and cultural background imaginable. They all had one important thing in common, the fear of their own coming death. You will learn how to biblically introduce the coming death of unsaved people, which is the start of the biblically strategized salvation gospel presentation. If you have unsaved family members and friends, they will respond to hearing this salvation gospel presentation for exactly the same reason. Do not pre-judge them, thinking you know them so well that you believe no salvation gospel presentation could ever impact them. Along the idea of pre-judging, it does not matter what an unsaved person thinks or claims to believe. No disrespect intended, but never let any unsaved person convince you that they know anything about biblically spiritual matters. They may try to convince you that they do, but do not let anything they say deter you from presenting this unique strategized salvation gospel presentation. The biblically strategized salvation gospel presentation is like no other and is your answer to lead them to Christ.

BE PREPARED TO WIN THEM NO MATTER WHO WHERE OR WHEN

In late July of 2019, two friends, both former Pastors, told me they were driving part time for Uber, it was uncomplicated while they did other things in their lives. They liked to drive earlier in the day, so the rest of the day was flexible. I'm an early riser, so driving part time to (LAX) Los Angeles International Airport early in the morning, worked for me and paid the best. I was working on this book and could move my writing schedule until later in the day. I ended up expanding my driving schedule, but driving for Uber, for the short that time I did, turned out to be a glorious experience.

I met a lot of very interesting people and led around three hundred (300) unsaved Uber riders to their decisions for Christ over a six month period of time. My brief part time Uber career ended when Covid hit in late January of 2020. These

Uber riding folks were all led to their decisions to accept Jesus Christ as their Savior, upon hearing exactly the same biblically strategized salvation gospel presentation that you are about to learn.

These Uber riders were from every background imaginable. They all heard exactly the same salvation gospel presentation and to them I was just a polite and friendly Uber driver. After basic introductions, some light conversation about where they were going and as the Lord led or impressed me, I told them that "I'm a Christian and I do evangelism work" to introduce or begin the biblically strategized salvation gospel presentation, with a calm voice and tone. As they listened to me, they too remained calm and they all followed along, word for word, as I led them to their decisions for Christ.

The Lord led me and I led them. It was that simple. With the exception of four or five, these salvations all took place while I drove and they were in the back seat of my car with minimal eye contact through the rearview mirror. With this gospel presentation, they all heard the need to accept Jesus Christ as their Savior in a way that they completely understood. After leading them to Christ, I referred many to churches that I knew of in the area's where they lived and encouraged them all to find a solid bible believing church.

NO MATTER WHERE YOU ARE THE LORD WANTS YOU IN GENTLE EVANGELISTIC CONTROL

After my season as a part time Uber driver ended, I understood exactly why the Lord led me to drive for Uber. It was to not only lead them to Christ, but also to share this "you will be prepared, because you will know what to say, to lead unsaved people to Christ anywhere and anytime" testimony with you. Over many years I have led countless numbers of unsaved people to Christ in many unusual situations and conditions. So, winning unsaved people to Christ while driving Uber may seem a bit different, but it really was not.

Once you learn what to say to lead any unsaved person to Christ with the biblically strategized salvation gospel presentation, you will know and understand how to evangelistically be able to be in control and know what you are doing at all times. It will not matter where you are or how "unusual" what happens to be going on around you may seem. The Lord will be with you and you will be the man, woman or mature teen in gentle evangelistic control of any interaction with an unsaved person. You, the Christian man, woman or mature teen, are the one called by the Lord, are the one to calmly and gently be in evangelistic control. This means you are the person always leading the evangelistic exchange, never an unsaved person. You will absolutely be prepared for any "unusual" situation that may come up. This testimony is also to encourage you to "not over think leading an unsaved person to Christ or where you may be when you lead them." Do not worry about or think you need some idealistically imagined, perfect situation or location in order to lead any unsaved person to Christ. When you are prepared and as the Spirit impresses or prompts you, you win them where you find them.

The most important and key factor in personal evangelism is always to know "what to say, why to say it, who to say it to, when to say it, where to say it and how to say it." This is exactly what the biblically strategized salvation gospel presentation will equip and prepare you to do. As the Lord leads, you too can lead unsaved family members, friends or strangers to their decision to accept Christ, anywhere, anytime, day or night.

WHAT YOU NEED TO SAY TO LEAD
UNSAVED PEOPLE TO CHRIST

In the process of learning this one of a kind salvation gospel presentation men, women and mature teens just like you, are going to learn precisely "what to say and why to say it, who to say it to, when to say it, where to say it and how to say it" in order to lead any unsaved person to their decision to immediately receive Jesus as their Savior. This unique salvation gospel presentation is easy to learn and present to any unsaved person, even if they live in another community, state or country. This is because with this gospel presentation it is just as easy to lead them to Christ on a telephone/cell, as it is in person.

A PREDICTABLE OUTCOME WHEN YOU
PRESENT THIS GOSPEL PRESENTATION

The predictable salvation outcome from what you are about to learn is that 95% to 100% of the unsaved people that hear this strategized salvation gospel presentation will immediately accept Jesus as Savior. On a year to year basis, these numbers may slightly vary from person to person, but the percentage of people receiving Christ is always extremely high. Some years every unsaved person that hears this salvation gospel presentation from you will receive Jesus as Savior. This is what the 100% figure represents. The differences in the percentage numbers are primarily from being accidently interrupted from an unavoidable distraction. When any unsaved person hears this one of a kind salvation gospel presentation it is very rare if they do not respond by immediately accepting Jesus as Savior.

TO BE PREPARED LEARN WHAT TO SAY

When you learn what to say, which is to learn the biblically strategized salvation gospel presentation. You will be fully prepared for personal evangelism and as you present this biblical gospel presentation, you will do so with an unstoppable assurance that you already know what the outcome is going to be, a salvation, a soul led and won to Christ.

To actually win souls in personal evangelism and not be limited to vague, general and often times, disconnected witnessing statements, there are two significant key components.

First, to be prepared for personal evangelism means to know what to say to introduce, present and conclude the salvation gospel to any unsaved person with a salvation result.

Second, to let the Holy Spirit or an Angel of the Lord lead or prompt you to the unsaved person that He wants you to present this gospel presentation to, no matter what the circumstances happen to be, in order to lead them to Christ.

SHOULD SALVATIONS ONLY TAKE PLACE IN CHURCH

In Acts 8:26-40, is the dramatic story that teaches not to be hesitant to lead an unsaved person to accept Jesus as their Savior outside of a church or church ministry. It is when Philip led the Ethiopian eunuch to Christ through personal evangelism inside a chariot/wagon.

Philip baptized him and "the Spirit of the Lord caught Philip away so the eunuch saw him no more." According to church tradition the eunuch went on to evangelize the African Continent.

You too, will lead someone to Christ that you will never see again. It could be on a airplane or a gas station parking lot. Pray for them and direct them to a church or denomination. You or I cannot possibly know what plan God has for any person when they accept Jesus Christ as their Savior.

CHAPTER TWO

THE MOST DAMAGING PROBLEMS
IN PERSONAL EVANGELISM

Throughout the body of Christ there are traditional personal evangelism terms and phrases that are familiar to most Christians. These familiar terms and phrases are "go witness, share your faith, share or give your testimony, share the Lord and build relationships with unsaved people in order to effectively witness to them or invite them to church." Most Christians generally understand what these evangelistic terms and phrases imply to go and do. The problem is that most Christians do not know what to say or do, in order to implement what these terms and phrases imply for them to go and do. Christians hear these traditional evangelism phrases, but rarely hear "go present the salvation gospel of Jesus Christ and win a soul." To present the salvation gospel implies and represents the intentional goal of leading an unsaved person to their decision for Christ.

WHY SO MANY FEEL THEY ARE ON THEIR OWN

To most Christians, the traditional personal evangelism phrases only imply doing something vague or general. This is because of little to no training on how to introduce, present and conclude sharing or presenting the salvation gospel with salvation results. Leaders tell non-clergy Christians to "trust the Lord for what to say." We must trust the Lord about everything in evangelism. As we do, it is best to already know what to say and be prepared for personal evangelism. Without knowing what to say in personal evangelism, most do little or nothing. The salvation gospel presentation that you will learn is the biblical solution to this massive personal evangelism problem. Presenting the biblically strategized salvation gospel presentation includes precisely what to say to introduce, present and conclude the salvation gospel with an immediate salvation result. It is the biblical way to learn how to lead or win unsaved people to Christ. This salvation gospel presentation will quickly give men, women and mature teens a high level of personal evangelism confidence that will last for the rest of their lives.

IN PERSONAL EVANGELISM THERE ARE CORE PROBLEMS

The core problems in personal evangelism are primarily from Christians not knowing "what to say" to unsaved people. Irrespective of church or denominational affiliation, individually there is wide spread fear, doubt and confusion. This comes from no personal direction, goal, structure, strategy or designed conclusion associated with "go witness, share your faith, share or give your testimony, share the Lord, build deep or meaningful relationships to effectively witness." Christians hear these evangelism encouragements and to many they are nothing more than idealistic evangelism ideas. The personal evangelism problem that has been continually destructive is that most Christians do not know "what to say" to unsaved people. They are trapped by fear, doubt and confusion from not knowing "what to say or saying the wrong thing." This creates the intimidating problem of not knowing "what to say to start or how to then end" any personal evangelism conversation. It does not matter what the topic of a conversation with an unsaved person may be, because the biblically strategized salvation gospel presentation always solves the "what to say next" problem. At the right time, it is designed to simply start the presentation, which will transition from any conversation with an unsaved person into this unique salvation gospel presentation and lead an unsaved person to their immediate decision to receive Jesus as their Savior.

CORE PROBLEMS ARE FROM UNFOCUSED OPTIONS

When Christians hear "go witness, share your faith, share or give your testimony, share the Lord and build deep relationships with unsaved people in order to effectively witness or invite them to church." The only part most Christians understand is invite them to church. The combination of all of these evangelism encouragements are extremely confusing to most Christians. Many Christians end up thinking something like: "What do they all mean and what should I say about them? I don't think I am supposed to witness, share my faith, share or give my testimony, share the Lord or say anything, unless I have a deep relationship with an unsaved person. What does that mean and how deep does it need to be? I only have a deep and meaningful relationship with my best friend. I have unsaved family members and friends and I've invited them to church, but they said no, they want to live their own life, so what do I do now? Does "witnessing" mean share my faith or give my testimony? It sounds like there are a bunch of rules that I don't understand. It is all a bit much, but then again, I really feel better letting more educated or qualified people do it, I hope someone will, because it's not for me."

Although this is a general observation it is actually fairly accurate. This is to help the body of Christ understand why most Christians do not participate in personal evangelism. Jesus Himself, simplified personal evangelism with one simple directive. Jn 4:38 He said "I sent you to reap that for which you have not labored, others have labored, and you have entered their labors." To reap means to lead or win an unsaved person to their decision for Christ. The traditional personal evangelism encouragements are all sowing processes not reaping processes. Reaping, leading or winning an unsaved person to Christ is exactly what you will learn how to do with the biblically strategized salvation gospel presentation.

CHRISTIANS ARE TOLD TO GO DO WHAT THEY DO NOT UNDERSTAND HOW TO GO DO

This is caused as a result of hearing evangelism terms and phrases that they do not understand how to move forward with and implement in any situation. It is the combination of these overwhelming evangelism realities that has practically destroyed personal evangelism ministry throughout the body of Christ. The solution to these personal evangelism problems for any Christian is this biblically strategized salvation gospel presentation. It is the answer to fulfill any personal evangelism need for a personal direction, goal, structure, strategy, conclusion and vision of what to say and do in personal evangelism. These are the fundamental reasons that most Christians are not prepared to engage in personal evangelism. Prov 28:18a "When there is no vision, the people perish." kjv. When men women and mature teens learn this unique salvation gospel presentation, they will then be prepared to engage in personal evangelism.

WHY YOU NEED THE BIBLICALLY STRATEGIZED SALVATION GOSPEL PRESENTATION

In Matt 13:19 Jesus states "When anyone hears the word of the kingdom and does not understand it, then the wicked one comes and snatches away what was sown in his heart. This is he who received seed by they wayside. In vs 23 He states "But he who received seed on the good ground is he who hears the word and understands it, who indeed bears fruit and produces: some a hundredfold, some sixty, some thirty."

Jesus is explaining that general or directionless witnessing without knowing specifically "what to say and why to say it, who to say it to, when to say it, where to say it and how to say it" that is understandable will lead to no salvation results. The strategized salvation gospel that you are about to learn is highly understandable and unsaved people completely understand what is presented to them and they will immediately accept and receive Jesus as their Savior. When Christians hear the traditional personal evangelism phrases with little or no training on how to introduce, present and conclude the salvation gospel of Jesus Christ, there is always doubt about what to say and do. Doubt is the breeding ground for confusion and fear. When Christians learn and present the biblically strategized salvation gospel presentation there is no doubt, confusion or fear about what to say and do in personal evangelism.

When Christians do not know what to say, most are confused, intimidated and do little to nothing in their personal evangelism. Witnessing attempts without this strategized salvation gospel presentation are like night and day. The biblically strategized salvation gospel presentation that you can easily learn is how to move a general witnessing conversation into introducing, presenting and conclude presenting the salvation gospel of Jesus Christ with an immediate salvation result. It will eliminate all fear, doubt and confusion in personal evangelism. This one of a kind salvation gospel presentation is the biblical way to prepare unsaved people to want to hear the salvation gospel and present it to them in a way that all unsaved people completely understand. This is vastly different than generalized witnessing or faith sharing with a logical or analytical sounding rationale, that has no goal, direction, structure or strategy to lead or win an unsaved person to receive Jesus as their Savior.

THEY DO NOT KNOW WHAT TO SAY

All Christians have heard these evangelistic phrases and many want to know the definition of "effective witnessing." Witnessing is a broadly and generally used evangelistic term with no specific identity or objective. It can also include all the other personal evangelism phrases and terms, because they too, are all general terms with no specificity of identity or objective. Using the term "effective" with witnessing, creates an elevated evangelism perception to it. A fundamental question that many have is how do you "effectively witness?" This is a profound sounding phrase that somehow implies that "effective witnessing" must be the gold standard of witnessing. For most Christians it has no practical applicable meaning, because ultimately, it could mean anything to anybody.

HOW AND WHY CHRISTIANS ARE
UNINTENTIONALY SET UP TO FAIL

Traditional evangelism phrases are evangelistic implications about what Christians should do in personal evangelism. They only imply what to do rather than specifically explaining exactly what to say or do in personal evangelism. To many Christians, even when they may have a sense of what these evangelism phrases imply to do evangelistically, but when out in the real world where the rubber meets the road evangelistically, they are functionally meaningless and directionless. This has led to millions of Christians being fearful and then passive. They are fearful and passive, because the traditional personal evangelism encouragements do not have a specific direction, goal, structure, strategy or conclusion. This is because without teaching on how to introduce, present and conclude the salvation gospel with an immediate salvation result, they have no personal evangelism confidence and end up evangelistically passive.

CHRISTIANS ARE UNINTENTIONALLY PUT IN A BOX

The most significant, but unintentional personal evangelism problem is from Christians being told to do something evangelistically, but with little to no training. They are told to go and do the traditional and historical evangelism phrases such as "go witness, share your faith, share your testimony, share the Lord, build relationships with unsaved people in order to effectively witness or invite to them to church", which are understood to mean to go and do something in personal evangelism. Over the years these encouragements have launched individual men, women and mature teens to reach out to unsaved people. As a result, many unsaved people, one way or another were led to Christ or invited to churches and were led to Christ through "alter calls, appeals or invitations to come forward to accept Jesus as Savior." These are all glorious events and moments in the history and story of the body of Christ, but in the 21st century, it is time to broaden personal evangelism vision. Unfortunately, in personal evangelism, around 95% of the body of Christ has never led or won an unsaved person to a decision for Christ.

This is because they are trapped in the box of fear, doubt and confusion about what to say or do in personal evangelism. It was certainly not intentional, but the traditional and historical personal evangelism encouragements with no specific training, unintentionally have had a negative impact on millions in the body of Christ. Without this specific kind of teaching and training, Christians are intimidated, negatively impacted and do little or nothing in person evangelism. Many sermons have focused on "thinking out of the box" and thinking out of the box is exactly what the biblically strategized salvation gospel presentation will do for you. It gives you precisely what to say and do that applies to every unsaved person.

LIMITED WITNESSING CAN NOW END

Throughout most of the 20th century, if an unsaved person was invited to visit a church, to many it was considered an honor and they would willingly attend. In the 21st century anti-Christ, anti-church culture of today, most unsaved people are not open to church visitation. With the biblically strategized salvation gospel presentation, Christians no longer have to be limited to the personal evangelism encouragements of "go witness, share your faith, share your testimony, share the Lord, build deep relationships in order to invite them to your church." To then invite family or friends as unsaved people, then hope and pray that they actually show up. If they show up, then hope and pray that someone else will led to Christ.

The result from only sharing general personal evangelism encouragements to unsaved people is that most Christians, to use a naval phrase, are "evangelistically, dead in the water." The biblically strategized salvation gospel presentation will instantly put "soulwinning wind into their evangelistic sails." This is another reason why the biblically strategized salvation gospel presentation is the personal evangelism game changer. It is for men, women and mature teens to know how to first lead an unsaved person to Christ and then invite them to their church, but as a new believer for discipleship and equipping to do the work of the ministry.

FREE FROM BEING TRAPPED BY FEAR

This is the freedom from being trapped in the box of fear, doubt and confusion in personal evangelism. When you learn this one of a kind salvation gospel presentation you will always know what you are going to say and do with an unsaved person. What is so encouraging and exciting is you will also already know what the unsaved person is going to say and do when you present this salvation gospel presentation. Keep in mind that with this salvation gospel presentation you control the words, the words do not control you. Once you learn the biblically strategized salvation gospel presentation, you will know what to say and do and then be free, free to be yourself. This is why pastors learn presentations, they call them sermons. Actors learn presentations, they call them scripts. Politicians learn presentations, they call them speeches. Salespeople learn presentations, they call them sales presentations. Teachers learn presentations, they call them lesson plans. These different kinds of presentations from these different kinds of people have one thing in common. Their various presentations all have a purpose and goal. The purpose and goal of the biblically strategized salvation gospel presentation is to lead or win unsaved people to an immediate decision to accept Jesus Christ as their Savior.

ANY FORM OF WITNESSING IS A PRESENTATION

It does not matter what an evangelistic encouragement is labeled or called. When a man, woman or mature teen is out in the real world evangelistically, whatever they say and how they say it to unsaved people, is their presentation. Once a Christian identifies himself or herself as a Christian, whatever a Christian tells an unsaved person is always a presentation.

Do not confuse presentation with a lack of sincerity. Evangelistic minded Christians should be aware that whatever they communicate with an unsaved person, no matter how miniscule, is always a presentation. You may ask, "does this mean I must always be wise about what I say to or around unsaved people?" Yes, because you are always waiting for the Lord to lead you to present the biblically strategized salvation gospel presentation.

Matt 10:16 "Behold, I send you out as sheep in the midst of wolves. Therefore be wise as serpents and harmless as doves."

THE DEEPEST PROBLEM WITH TRADITIONAL
WITNESSING IS THAT IT IS TO SOW NOT TO REAP

A lot of personal evangelism encouragement throughout the body of Christ is based upon "a maybe or something could possibly happen", with little hope to accomplish a salvation result. It is to evangelistically "settle for less". Christians are told to "go witness, share your faith, give your testimony, share the Lord, build deep relationships with unsaved people", but to what end? The answer is there is no end, other than "a maybe, a possibility or hoped for end and keep praying." These general witnessing processes are generally to prepare unsaved people to possibly be led or won to Christ at a later time and probably by another Christian. These are classic evangelism encouragements to sow seeds to be possibly harvested or reaped at a later time, place or event. The deep personal evangelism problem is that what these evangelism phrases and words imply to do, is actually the exact opposite of what Jesus Himself stated that He wants the body of Christ to go and do. Jesus in John 4:35 stated "I sent you to reap that for which you have not labored, others have labored, and you have entered into their labors." In a later chapter you will learn in great detail what Jesus told the body of Christ to do in evangelism.

EFFECTIVE WITNESSING IS SUPPORTIVE
LOW KEY AND GENERAL

Effective witnessing should always be low-key, never intimidating, argumentative or controversial. It should have simple and uncomplicated references to the things of God awaiting, for the right Spirit led moment to present the strategized salvation gospel presentation. In other words, "effective witnessing" should not create attitudes, arguments or controversy that can get in the way of leading an unsaved person to Christ. You a Christian, are yourself an "effective lifestyle witness" and may be the only bible some unsaved people have ever read. You are a living and walking epistle, showing the Christ in you. You simply need to be who God has made you to be, no one else and as you trust in Him, even strangers will recognize the Christ in you.

2Cor3:2-3 "You are our epistle written in our hearts known and read by all men; clearly you are an epistle of Christ, ministered by us, written not with ink but by the Spirt of the living God, non on tablets of stone but on tablets of flesh, that is, of the heart."

THE KEY TO EFFECTIVE WITNESSING IS TO ALREADY KNOW WHAT TO SAY

The key to understand "effective witnessing" is simple. It is to already know "what to say and why to say it, who to say it to, when to say it, where to say it and how to say it" in order to lead any unsaved person to their immediate decision to accept Jesus as their Savior. When you learn these things, which you will, when you learn the strategized salvation gospel presentation, you can then approach any witnessing or general conversation with an unsaved person with a calm assurance. This is because you will know exactly what is going on and will be able to pace, adapt, adjust or change the direction of any conversation into the salvation gospel presentation. This is because you are always waiting on the Lord to lead or prompt you to start the biblically strategized salvation gospel presentation. The most effective witnessing is simple and minimal. It should not open a door to controversial subjects as you wait on the Lord to lead you to present this salvation gospel presentation.

"Effective witnessing is not the key to leading unsaved people to decisions for Christ. It is the ability to lead unsaved people to decisions for Christ that is the key to effective witnessing."

Brent Price

CHAPTER THREE

HAVE YOU ASKED A LEADER WHAT TO SAY TO AN UNSAVED PERSON

Have you ever asked a church leader or another Christian the following question or a variation of it? "My brother, my friend or my mother is unsaved and I have been trying to witness to him/her and don't seem to get anywhere. What should I say to him/her?" Many years ago, before I knew how to lead unsaved people to Christ, I asked a pastor a similar question and at another time, overheard someone else ask the exact same question. The answers to the both of us were almost identical. The answers were "I don't know them and everyone is different, so I don't know what you should say to them, just continue to pray for them and witness to them."

STOP VIEWING UNSAVED PEOPLE IN THE FLESH

On the surface that may sound like a reasonable and rational response, but actually, it is a worldly answer based upon a fleshly view of people. In the world people are judged and put in identity boxes based on their personality, the work they do, their race, whether they are male or female, their hair or eye color, young or old, social or academic status and this analysis could go on and on. This worldly mindset is also how an enormous portion of the body of Christ evangelically perceives, views or thinks it understands unsaved people. Traditionally, most personal evangelism or "Relational Evangelism" thinking has been limited to promoting church invitation or the absolute need to create a deep relationship with an unsaved person in order to discover a "hot button issue or need" to effectively witness to them. This is the historical general personal evangelism mindset based on the relational capabilities between Christians and unsaved people. No matter how sincere the encouraging intent, an exclusive relational driven, personal evangelism model, generally has little to no teaching or training on how to introduce, present and conclude the salvation gospel, with an immediate salvation result. The biblically strategized salvation gospel presentation, balanced with a relational evangelism mindset, will prepare Christians to lead any unsaved person to Christ. This balanced combination is the answer and solution to every personal evangelism question, challenge and problem.

EVERYONE SEEMS TO BE DIFFERENT BUT THEY ARE NOT

Most Christians are trapped in a vacuum of uncertainty about what to say to an unsaved person. They are trapped, because they have been taught to believe they have to witness or interact with an unsaved person with a creative or original witnessing concept, tailored to the individual needs or personality of an unsaved person. Many Christians think they need to endlessly search for the "current personal problem or hot button need" of an unsaved person. Many have been taught to do this so they can "figure out" what to say in order to explain how Jesus Christ can solve their problem. Most of the body of Christ seems to think that the "hot button" needs are generally in the area of "work, relationships, addiction issues, marriage problems or marital status, health problems, lack of church attendance, perhaps being unsaved or other obvious life challenges."

DEVELOP DEEP RELATIONSHIPS FIND FELT NEEDS INVITE TO CHURCH ARE TRADITIONAL

A lot of general witnessing is trying to convince an unsaved person that Jesus can solve their personal problems. Historically, the main goal in personal evangelism is not to win souls, but to build relationships with unsaved people to ultimately invite them to church. The hope is unsaved people will relate to church life, have needs met or find the solution to their problem and perhaps receive the Lord if an invitation to receive Christ is offered. A felt need could be any situation that is impacting an unsaved person or it can be as simple as a Christian being helpful in an obvious immediate need. However, He did not go to the cross to solve personal problem's, He came to save people from their sin problem. He can of course solve worldly problems, but when an evangelism focus is on Jesus solving general life problems, to unsaved people this can easily sound like Jesus is just another self-help guru option to potentially solve life issues and problems. Unsaved people are completely incapable of understanding what He can do to solve all of their problems. Many in the body of Christ assume or think that solving obvious life problems is what appeals to unsaved people. They think or believe that getting relationally close on these personal issues will cause unsaved people to want to take their advice to accept Jesus as their Savior, visit their church and ultimately solve a current problem.

FOCUS ON WHAT JESUS WILL DO FOR THEM NOT WHAT HE DID FOR YOU

Some believe the appeal that Jesus can eventually solve personal life problems is what unsaved people want to hear about what Jesus Christ can do. In the broadest evangelism view, there have been many unsaved people that have been led to Jesus as their Savior with a "hot button, felt need focus." This is the traditional personal evangelism focus that has been handed down from one Christian generation to the next for decades. It sounds or feels like a logical or rational thing to focus on in a general witnessing process. The "personal testimony witnessing perception" is if a Christian is excited, happy and feels blessed about what God did in their lives, then everyone else will also be just as excited, including unsaved people. This is always the case when something wonderful that the Lord has done in a Christians life is shared in Sunday School, home group or in any setting with other Christians. In the world with unsaved people it can be just a religious story, because it can easily sound like "it's all about me, myself and I, a witnessing Christian."

TIME TO MOVE BEYOND TRADITION

Many years ago, when I was a bible college student, I took a course on "Evangelism." The course focus was identifying and explaining evangelism terms that were in the context of church mission. This included the meaning of "The Great Commission." The conclusion was that the church evangelism mission foundation was for Christians to always be "salt and light." Matt 5:13-16a "You are the salt of the earth. You are the light of the world. Let your light so shine." The personal evangelism mission has historically and traditionally been centered around "inviting and encouraging unsaved people to visit the local church." The hopeful goal is for them to receive Jesus as their Savior. This could happen as a result of an "invitation" to come forward to receive Christ or have some demonstration or signal that an unsaved person was receiving Christ. It could be "a raised hand or a looking up from a bowed head." Unfortunately, in many churches this opportunity does not take place. In the "church invitation model" there is the hope of church members reaching out in a welcoming manner to encourage unsaved people to return and become part of the local church fellowship. The traditional or historical evangelism emphasis has been focused on church invitation in personal evangelism, not winning unsaved people to Christ in personal evangelism.

THE EXCLUSIVE CHURCH INVITATION MODEL
HAS ALWAYS HAD A NEGATIVE SIDE TO IT

A negative side of the "church invitation model" is that it takes time to develop the "idealistically perfect relationship" with an unsaved person to have them actually respond and visit your church. The problem is that unsaved people die naturally or are killed one way or another, before they actually visit a church. Before unsaved people receive Christ or visit a witnessing Christian's church, they also can move to another job location, another community, be recruited by a more aggressive cult or false religion member and for these reasons and more, leave a witnessing Christian's life. The overall view of "church invitation ministry" is that if an unsaved person visits a church, there is hopefully an "attempt by someone to evangelize the already partially evangelized." Realistically, if an unsaved person has been "evangelized", this should mean that they have actually been won to their decision for Christ.

Church invitation as the "preferred evangelism model" has many unknown's and is always reliant on other Christians, who may or may not know what they are doing, that minister to unsaved people as a church visitor. At the conclusion of the Bible College Evangelism Course, the professor stated "if you want to win a soul, you will have to figure out for yourself what to say to an unsaved person." The good new's here is that no one needs to try and "figure out" what to say to unsaved people, because this is exactly what the biblically strategized salvation gospel presentation provides for men, women and mature teens throughout the body of Christ. Don't forget that the results of a "hot button, felt need, church invitation emphasis" are that around 95% of all Christians have never led a single unsaved person to accept and receive Jesus as their Savior.

UNSAVED PEOPLE NEED A STRONG "REASON WHY" THEY SHOULD ACCEPT AND RECEIVE JESUS AS THEIR SAVIOR

One of the critically important reasons that most Christians have never led an unsaved person to Christ is not giving unsaved people a powerful or strong enough "reason why" to accept and receive Jesus as Savior. This is from having little to no direction, goal, structure or strategy in witnessing and as a result, do not know "what to say, why to say it, who to say it to, when to say it, where to say it or how to say it to an unsaved person, that understandably gives them a "reason why" that they need to accept and receive Jesus as their Savior. All of humanity needs a "reason why" to do anything significant in life and receiving Jesus Christ as Savior is the most significant event of life. In personal evangelism most particularly, there must be a powerful, strong and understandable "reason why" for an unsaved person to want to accept and receive Jesus as Savior. Unsaved people need to hear a "reason why" that makes sense to them personally. They need to hear a strong "reason why" that they can relate to, understand and realize that the need to immediately receive Christ is for them personally. This is exactly what the strategized salvation gospel presentation will do.

WITNESSING WITH NO STRONG REASON WHY IS WEAK

If a Christian relies on telling an unsaved person that Jesus Christ will "possibly or potentially help them with different life issues, because He helped me, a witnessing Christian", then they will be very limited. This witnessing concept and gospel presentation based upon "a potential possibility for the unsaved" is not a powerful or strong enough "reason why" on its own, for an unsaved person to make a decision for Christ. A personal testimony can easily sound as if it is "all about me, myself and I", which can be difficult for an unsaved person to understandably relate to and comprehend "how, what or why" the Lord did for another person. Many unsaved people have and will respond to that form of witnessing and other general witnessing statements and come to Christ. On a large evangelistic scale, trying to train millions throughout the body of Christ, with these witness type attempts to win souls has historically has been extremely unsuccessful. This is because these witnessing type attempts, simply do not have a powerful enough "reason why" for unsaved people to accept Jesus as their Savior, because they are only sowing attempts.

THE BIBLICALLY STRATEGIZED SALVATION GOSPEL PRESENTATION IS ABOUT THEM NOT YOU

When men, women and mature teens learn and present the biblically strategized salvation gospel presentation, 95% to 100% of the unsaved people that hear it, immediately accept and receive Jesus as their Savior. This is because the biblically strategized salvation gospel presentation is designed to focus on Jesus Christ, the salvation and eternal life of an unsaved person. It is not designed to talk about or refer to the "me, myself and I" of personal testimony. Salvation, death and eternal life without a doubt become the greatest needs and concerns that all unsaved people have when they hear this one of a kind salvation gospel presentation. When unsaved people hear the biblically strategized salvation gospel presentation, they not only hear it, but they completely understand it and will immediately respond to it. This is because they are hearing the most powerful "reason why" that they have ever heard for them to make their decision to immediately accept and receive Jesus as Savior.

NO ONE UNDERSTANDS UNTIL THEY RECEIVE JESUS AS THEIR SAVIOR

Unsaved people will not begin to understand all He can do until they have first been led to receive Him as their Savior and become born again. Trying to explain to an unsaved person what Jesus can do in a person's life is kind of like trying to explain "what chocolate ice cream tastes like, to a person who has never had ice cream." General witnessing that focuses on what He can potentially do after salvation is like "putting the cart before the horse." This is a huge contributor as to why many may witness, but very few actually lead an unsaved person to a decision to receive Jesus as their Savior. This evangelism worldview is based upon the perceived individuality or uniqueness of every individual unsaved person. It comes from a worldly assumption that everyone's needs are completely different, which is true on many issues other than coming death.

STOP THINKING INDIVIDUALITY ALL UNSAVED PEOPLE ARE EXACTLY ALIKE

The common thread that weaves all unsaved people together and is what makes them all exactly the same is their uncertainty, insecurity and fear about their coming death. Unsaved people, no matter what kind of impressive academic, social or professional image they put forth, have no understanding or assurance about what happens at death. They all know death is coming and have probably never discussed their own coming death other than conversations with an insurance agent. They are all deeply conflicted about their eternal destination. They do not know what death will mean to them. This fear of coming death and what it leads to or means to them is what makes every unsaved person identical and exactly the same.

ALL UNSAVED PEOPLE ARE INSECURE ABOUT DEATH

Several years ago, a movie star, now deceased, was a member of the Beverly Hills Community Church, that I pastored for 22 years. She knew Jesus as her Savior and she shared with me about a former husband, another movie star, then deceased. She was married to him before she came to Christ. I knew who he was as an actor and he was always in "strong, tough guy" roles. She shared with me that he was unsaved and how fearful he was of death. She said he lived his life, "literally scared to death" of death. She told me that she never heard of him coming to Christ. The wealth, position or status of any unsaved person does not matter. All unsaved people are internally insecure and scared about death.

I have referred to leading wealthy or well known successful sounding people to Christ for only one reason. It is to encourage men, women and mature teens that it does not matter what the life status or financial circumstances are of any unsaved person. When it comes to their own coming death, rich or poor, they are all the same. Irrespective if they voice it or not, they are all insecure and fearful about coming death.

Many Christians only feel secure witnessing when they themselves feel superior to an unsaved person. An unsaved person may have to be emotionally tramatized, in a lesser financial situation or lesser job status position for some Christians to feel secure enough to reach out to them. All of those fearful and insecure issues about reaching out to any unsaved person, rich or poor, will end when you learn the biblically strategized salvation gospel presentation. Mk 8:36 "For what will it profit a man if he gains the whole world, and loses his own soul?"

COMING DEATH IS THE ULTIMATE "HOT BUTTON" FOR ALL UNSAVED PEOPLE

The coming death of every unsaved person is the ultimate "Hot Button" and why they can easily be led to Christ. The initial subject focus of the biblically strategized salvation gospel presentation is death, the coming death of an unsaved person. As you will learn, this is the subject focus that the bible clearly teaches to emphasize and target in order to lead or win an unsaved person to Christ. It is their deep lack of knowledge about what comes after death and their God given desire to want eternal life in heaven, which makes them available to immediately be led to pray to receive Jesus as Savior. What will be new to an unsaved person is how they are gently being questioned about their own coming death in this salvation gospel presentation. The biblically strategized salvation gospel presentation is designed to introduce and explain the eternal danger of their coming death in a way that they will hear and completely understand. They will then immediately want to accept Jesus as their Savior to be eternally safe in heaven with Him.

COMING DEATH IS WHAT IS MOST IMPORTANT TO UNSAVED PEOPLE

I have had Christians tell me and heard others say something like "I had a deep and penetrating conversation about the things of God with an unsaved person. I think the unsaved person heard new things and I know I powerfully informed him/her about the things of God." In every situation, they did not lead the unsaved person to Christ, but they "knew" the unsaved person powerfully heard "about the things of God." Granted the unsaved person could eventually go to a church and get saved or possibly pray to receive Jesus as their Savior on their own. In the meantime, if they die in a car wreck, have a heart attack and die, what good to them was hearing a "deep and penetrating conversation about the things of God" if they were not won to Christ? Unsaved people die and at any moment. This is why it is so important to be prepared to win any unsaved person to Christ at a moment's notice. The biblically strategized salvation gospel presentation will prepare you to win any unsaved person to Christ at a moments notice. Matt 10:16 "Behold, I send you out as sheep in the midst of wolves. Therefore be wise as serpents and harmless as doves."

"The world defines success many ways, but the greatest success of life is leaving this life alive in Jesus Christ."

Brent Price

CHAPTER FOUR

MILLIONS ARE ALREADY SOWED NOW IS THE TIME TO REAP THEM

Logically thinking, to sow is to wait for a potential future harvest. To reap is to immediately bring in the harvest. To reap, according to Jesus Himself, is to lead or win an unsaved person to receive Jesus Christ as Savior. This is the season and time like no other, to harvest the unsaved in America and the world in the name of Jesus Christ. This is because there are now untold millions of unsaved men, women, boys and girls that are already aware that Jesus Christ died on the cross. They have already had Jesus Christ sowed into them. How many unsaved people do you know that have never heard about Jesus death on the cross? I can tell you exactly how many you know, none. So then, just "what would you say" if you ever do encounter an unsaved person who has never heard of Jesus Christ? The biblically strategized salvation gospel presentation is absolutely "what to say" in order to present Him, explain Him and win them to Him. You will absolutely know what to say to win them to Christ. Unsaved people are aware of and have heard from many different sources that He suffered, died on the cross and arose on the third day. They do not understand why He had to go to the cross and that He did it for them personally.

UNSAVED PEOPLE ALREADY HAVE
CHRIST SOWED INTO THEM

The mere presence of a church sows Jesus Christ into an unsaved person. Christmas and Resurrection Sunday (Easter) both mightily sow Jesus Christ into the lives of unsaved people. Jesus Christ is already a reality to most unsaved people. They have heard about Him all of their lives. Many unsaved people have visited a church during Christmas or Easter and sung or listened to "Joy to the world or Up from the Grave He Arose" and many other songs praising Jesus Christ. Most say "Merry Christmas" during the Christmas season. Some say "Happy Holidays", but they still know Christmas is part of the greeting.

STOP THINKING SOW AND START THINKING REAP

In a historical or academic context, unsaved people already accept at some level, that what is told about Jesus Christ is true, that He is real to others and going to church is good, but it is just not yet true or real to them personally. They want Him, but have no idea how to express that want or need, but it is in them all. This is why unsaved people need to be led or won to Christ. They simply need a prepared man, woman or mature teen to understandably explain Him to them with the biblically strategized salvation gospel presentation. Unsaved people, except in certain areas of the world, are constantly reminded, one way or another, of Jesus Christ and that He died on the cross. Most Christians have heard a leader or someone say "unsaved people see something special in them and they want it." This is absolutely true. Unsaved people do not understand what they think they see and they are easy to relate to and can easily be led to receive Him with this salvation gospel presentation. They are drawn, want to be friendly or relate to you, because of the Christ in you. Jesus knew that in the 21st Century that this would be the evangelism reality and opportunity. The biblically strategized salvation gospel presentation gives men, women and mature teens the training, equipping and ability to now become reapers. To reap is what "make disciples, harvesting, winning souls or leading to Christ," all mean.

ALMOST ALL UNSAVED ARE READY NOW TO RECEIVE JESUS AS THEIR SAVIOR

Almost all unsaved people, except those in very isolated places, know a lot about Jesus Christ. Almost every unsaved person already has a good and positive sense or feeling about Jesus Christ. Jesus has consistently been deeply sown into them throughout their lives. He is a reality in their lives, whether they understand it or not. The unsaved simply do not understand how or why what He did on the cross means to them personally. The biblically strategized salvation gospel presentation will put it all together for them and they will immediately receive Him as their Savior. Christians should never think that unsaved people are not willing to hear the salvation gospel of Jesus Christ. They all are, they just do not know it yet or voice it. All unsaved people, except for those in remote locations, know that He went to the cross.

All of their lives, unsaved people have heard that He was crucified on the cross. What they do not know or understand is why He had to go the cross for all of humanity. The unsaved do not understand that He went to the cross especially for them. Every unsaved person needs a personal evangelism prepared man, woman or mature teen to explain to them precisely why He had to be crucified. His crucifixion, to have meaning for an unsaved person, has to be explained in way that they understand was for them personally. This is exactly and completely what the biblically strategized salvation gospel presentation will do.

UNSAVED PEOPLE HAVE MORE INTEREST IN JESUS CHRIST AND ETERNAL LIFE THAN THEY REVEAL

At times unsaved people publicly state that they have no interest in Christ. Even when they say that, they are inwardly interested in the full story of why He went to the cross. Do not think that just because you have not observed or heard of them openly pursuing answers about why He went to the cross, that it somehow implies or means that they do not want to hear and know the complete story of why He went to the cross.

This is because all unsaved people, and again except those in remote areas, have heard that what He did on the cross had something to do with how to go to heaven. All unsaved people, no matter who they are, have either spoken or unspoken deep and fearsome questions about death. They want to know what it will mean to themselves. The biblically strategized salvation gospel presentation will give them all of the answers they want and need about death and eternal life. What all unsaved people need is a personal evangelism prepared man, woman or mature teen to present the biblically strategized salvation gospel presentation, which will explain what he did on the cross for them personally.

JESUS SAYS REAP PAUL SAYS WIN THE BODY OF CHRIST SAYS SOW

The traditional evangelism encouragements to "go witness, share your faith, give your testimony, share the Lord, build relationships to effectively witness or to invite to church" are all sowing processes, not reaping or harvesting processes. In 1Cor 9:19 the Apostle Paul stated "For though I am free from all men, I have made myself a servant to all, that I might win the more." Jesus Himself, in the book of John 4:38, clearly stated "I sent you to reap that for which you have not labored, others have labored and you have entered into their labors." For many years, even though Jesus said "I sent you to reap", most of the body of Christ has been focused on promoting sowing through traditional evangelism encouragements.

JESUS CHRIST STATED THAT HE WANTS REAPERS NOT SOWERS

After the Great Commission, the scriptures in John 4:1-42 are the most important evangelism scriptures in the bible. It is here, that Jesus Himself, proclaims and establishes how He wants the body of Christ to evangelistically think, be aware of and awaken to in order to be prepared to fulfill the Great Commission. His mission here is to establish evangelistic thinking, particularly personal evangelism thinking, from a sowing mindset into a reaping mindset. A reaping mindset, attitude and goal can only come from being prepared to immediately win or lead unsaved people to accept Jesus as the Savior and receive Him as their own Savior. He also establishes that He will only give "a wage for reaping, but none for sowing." Some may refer to "a wage as a reward." No one knows exactly what "wage or reward" means or how it is manifested, but whatever it is, every Christian will be blessed to receive it. How and when the Lord chooses to bless you with His wage is all in His hands, but there is only one way to get your wage and that is to start leading or winning unsaved people to Christ.

JESUS CHRIST KNOWS WHAT HE IS DOING

In the book of John is the story of when Jesus Christ met the Samaritan woman at the well. It was to this woman that Jesus revealed Himself to be the Messiah. He did this for a specific reason. He always knew what He was doing and why He was doing it. He revealed Himself as the Messiah, because He knew how she would react to what He was telling her. Her predictable reaction to this glorious revelation was to go around the city telling the men about Jesus and what He revealed and said to her. The reaction of the men in the Samaritan city of Sychar was just as predictable. Jesus knew that they would want to come to Him.

UNSAVED PEOPLE RECEIVE JESUS WHEN
THEY ARE READY TO HEAR ABOUT HIM

The men from Sychar were role model types for all unsaved people who have heard about Messiah/Jesus and are available, willing and want to hear more about Him. They wanted to know more about the Man who told this local woman things about her and that He was the coming Messiah. The woman at the well may not have intended to, but she led some to Christ and got others excited enough to want to go find and meet Him. The woman at the well would have very excitedly told the men about her encounter with this Man that she perceived was a prophet and that He revealed Himself as the Messiah. She shared that He told her things about herself and hearing all of this caused the men from Sychar to immediately stop whatever they were doing to go out to Him. They also wanted to meet Him and find out for themselves the truth about this Man who declared Himself to be the Messiah. Jesus Christ Himself, used the woman at the well to do a great work.

JESUS UNIQUELY USED THE WOMAN AT THE WELL

At the time, the Samaritan woman at the well, would not have understood what she was doing, but the Lord used her to do a mighty work. Through her, men, women and mature teens, can see that it doesn't take a biblical scholar to lead unsaved people to decisions for Christ. The woman at the well had flaws, just as all of humanity has flaws. Every person has flaws when they receive Jesus as Savior. All Christians, including myself, are in a perpetual growing process and He always uses Christians with flaws, just like us to do His will.

JESUS REVEALED HIMSELF TO THE WOMAN AT THE WELL TO ESTABLISH A NEW WAY TO THINK

Jesus intentionally revealed Himself as the Messiah to the woman at the well to ultimately make his clear statement on how He wants the body of Christ to evangelistically think about sowing and reaping. He is about to establish a new evangelism mindset of reaping as the evangelism mindset, attitude and priority, not sowing. It was new then and still is today. The world logically thinks it must sow before it can reap and so does most of the body of Christ. He is using a sowing and reaping model to teach the body of Christ to reverse how to think evangelistically about sowing and reaping. His goal was to establish reaping as the personal evangelism priority, not sowing.

John 4:31-38 "In the meantime His disciples urged Him, saying, "Rabbi eat." But He said to them, I have food to eat of which you do not know." Therefore the disciples said to one another, "Has anyone brought Him anything to eat?" Jesus said to them, "My food is to do the will of Him who sent Me, and to finish His work. "Do you not say, "There are still four months and then comes the harvest"? Behold, I say to you, lift up your eyes and look at the fields, for they are already white for harvest! "And he who reaps receives wages and gathers fruit for eternal life, that both he who sows and he who reaps may rejoice together. 'For in this the saying is true: "One sows and another reaps.' "I sent you to reap that for which you have not labored; others have labored, and you have entered into their labors."

JESUS STATES IF YOU ONLY SOW I WILL NOT GIVE YOU A WAGE

In John 4:36, Jesus may have been addressing His disciples, but He is speaking to the body of Christ. When He explains that the fields that are white for harvest, He is referring to the unsaved men from Sychar that He sees are coming to meet Him. He uses them metaphorically to represent all unsaved people that are hungry for Him, whether they realize it or not. The men from the city were hungry for Him and represent the world that is also hungry for Him, but just do not know or understand it yet. He uses them as an illustration to strongly emphasize that reapers participate in three things. (1) He states that reapers "receive wages." (2) He then states that reapers "gather fruit for eternal life." (3) He concludes vs 36, by stating that "he who sows and he who reaps may rejoice together." The reality is that all Christians rejoice whenever they hear of an unsaved person receiving Jesus as Savior. He is powerfully stating that if a Christian only sows, they get no wage.

In vs 37, He states "For in this the saying is true: 'One sows and another reaps.' In vs 38, He states "I sent you to reap that for which you have not labored; others have labored, and you have entered into their labors."

THIS GOSPEL PRESENTATION IS TO REAP AND THE RESULTS ARE PREDICTABLE

Jesus Himself is strongly proclaiming that He wants the evangelism focus on reaping, not sowing. He is not saying to never sow, but to adjust evangelism thinking to become a reaper not just a sower. Keep in the mind that in the process of reaping evangelistically, you automatically sow. Anytime Jesus Christ is presented in order to reap, there is always sowing. This is why He calls the body of Christ to pray for laborers to go into His harvest that can reap, not sow. The reaction of the woman at the well was predictable. The reaction of the men from Sycar was predictable. The reaction of unsaved people that you present this biblically strategize salvation gospel presentation to is predictable. When unsaved people hear this uniquely strategized salvation gospel presentation, 95% to 100% of those that hear it, immediately accept and receive Jesus as their Savior. When

Christian's are not prepared and do not know "what to say and why to say it, who to say it to, when to say it, where to say it and how to say it" to unsaved people, what they do is also predictable. They do nothing.

Jesus in Luke 10:2 declares, "The harvest truly is great, but the laborers are few; therefore pray the Lord of the harvest to send out laborers into His harvest." In the 21st century, except in isolated locations, Jesus Christ has been sowed into the world. Most of the world has heard about Him all of their lives, but do not understand why they need to accept Him as their Savior.

No matter if personal evangelism is labeled as witnessing, sharing faith or sharing testimony, they all have to be communicated by speaking words. When you learn the words of this salvation gospel presentation you will be prepared to reap.

21ST CENTURY CHRISTIANS "WAKE UP AND SMELL THE COFFEE" IT'S TIME TO REAP THEY'VE ALREADY BEEN SOWED

In John 4:35, Jesus makes a rhetorical statement to His disciples "Do you not say four months and then comes" the Harvest"? He makes this statement as He observes the townsmen from Sychar, that the Samaritan woman at the well told vs29 "Come see a Man who told me all things that I ever did. Could this be the Christ?" Jesus, then says to His disciples "Behold, I say to you, lift up your eyes and look at the fields, for they are already white for harvest!" The point is don't sow them again, reap them.

When Jesus uses the word "Behold", He is telling them that He wants them to take notice. He is letting the disciples know that what He is about to say is highly significant. Jesus is declaring that the disciples and the body of Christ in the 21st century need to look at the unsaved with new eyes. Stop looking at them as someone who has to be sowed, so 21st century

Christians, "wake up and smell the coffee", it's time to reap, they've already been sowed.

The woman at the well sowed Christ to the townsmen and He is saying to His disciples and also to the body of Christ, particularly in the 21st century, stop thinking unsaved people have to be sowed over and over, again and again. They are ready to be reaped now, so reap them, which means to lead them to their decision for Christ. This is what the biblically strategized salvation gospel presentation will equip and prepare you to do.

IN PERSONAL EVANGLISM MOST OF THE BODY OF CHRIST IS SOWER MINDED NOT REAPER MINDED

Keep in mind that the men from Sychar were drawn to Christ with only a very excitable, but glorious personal testimony. It was powerful enough that they wanted more about Jesus. They wanted more and so they immediately dropped whatever they were doing and went to Jesus Himself.

Unsaved men, women, boys and girls today are just as easy to win to Christ as were those men 2000 years ago. In most of the world, except in remote areas everyone already knows a lot about Jesus. They have all been sowed to Christ from endless sources. They are ready and willing to be reaped.

Most Christians have heard "go witness, share your faith, give your testimony, invite an unsaved person to church and so on" over and over, again and again. These traditional phrases are only about sowing, not reaping. With this gospel presentation you can now change your limited personal evangelism thinking from "all I can do is witness to I now know how to reap." In other words, "it's time to wake up and smell the coffee."

EVERYONE UNSAVED PERSON YOU ENCOUNTER
HAS ALREADY BEEN SOWED TO CHRIST

In the 21st century with extremely few exceptions, unsaved people have already been sowed to Christ from many sources. They are now ready and willing to be reaped or led to Christ. The limited and directionless focus on sowing is why around 95% of the body of Christ has never led a single soul to Christ. They have been told over and over again through traditional personal evangelism phrases like "go witness", which really means "go sow and go sow some more."

Most Christians are confused, intimidated, afraid and have no idea what to say to lead an unsaved person to Christ. As a result, on the inside are screaming in frustration, pain and guilt over not being able to lead unsaved family members, friends and occasional strangers to Christ.

As a man, woman or mature teen does witness in a general or low-key way or just have a general conversation with an unsaved person, they will now know what to do. By taking the time to learn and know this gospel presentation, they will then know exactly what to do. They will then know how to easily transition into presenting the full biblically strategized salvation gospel with a salvation result.

ANY FARMER WILL TELL YOU THERE IS A
RIGHT WAY AND A WRONG WAY TO REAP

It does not matter which crop a farmer is growing. They will all tell you there is a right way and a wrong way to bring in their crop or reap their harvest. I grew up in Lockhart, Texas and one summer several of my friends and I worked for a local farmer for a short period of time "pulling broomcorn." Broomcorn is a stalk plant that looks like a normal corn plant. The difference is at the top there is about 18 inches or more of wisp, which is where broom wisp's come from.

Before we started, we were trained. We were taught how to reach up and grab the bottom of the wisp stalk and pull it down. This would produce a short thin stalk with the wisp attached. After pulling 6-8 wisp stalk's, we were to place them on the ground a certain way for stalk pickers to retrieve as we went down our row.

The training was very precise. If done wrong, a crop would be minimized or lost. Reaping a harvest is a precise event, not a "que sera sera" event. A farmer wants his or her crop harvested the right way in order to have a good crop for the marketplace.

In personal evangelism there is a right way and a wrong way to labor and reap in His harvest. Most of the body of Christ has been trying to fulfill the Great Commission with a sowing mindset and sowing phrases, not realizing that almost all of the unsaved world has already been sowed to Christ.

THE ERA OF REAPING IN PERSONAL EVANGELISM HAS COME

After the Great Depression of the 1930's and World War ll in the 1940's, unsaved people in the millions were invited to churches and they joyfully flocked to attend. In the 21st century, this is not the case. Most of the body of Christ's personal evangelism thinking is still from that earlier era. So, Christians today hear a lot of "go witness and invite to church." The truth is with this biblically strategized salvation gospel presentation, it is much easier to first lead them to Christ and then invite them to your church or a Christian fellowship as a new believer in Jesus Christ.

Mid 20th century personal evangelism thinking is why around 95% of the body of Christ has never won a single soul to Christ. Just like a farmer wants his or her crop harvested correctly, Jesus Christ wants His harvest harvested correctly. He wants laborers that are trained and know how to reap in His harvest.

The only way to do that is "not to focus on go witness, but focus on go reap", which means lead unsaved family members, friends or occasional strangers to their immediate decision to accept Jesus Christ as their Savior. This can and will happen as men, women and mature teens learn the biblically strategized salvation gospel presentation. The world has been sowed to Jesus Christ and are ready and willing to be reaped, which means to be led to their decision for Him in His glorious harvest.

ALMOST ALL OF THE WORLD IS SOWED
THE 21ST CENTURY IS THE TIME TO REAP

The bible declares in Rev 14:14-16 "Then I looked and behold, a white cloud, and on the cloud sat One like the Son of Man, having on His head a golden crown, and in His hand a sharp sickle. And another angel came out of the temple, crying with a loud voice to Him who sat on the cloud, "Trust in Your sickle and reap for the time has come for You to reap, for the harvest of the earth is ripe." So He who sat on the cloud thrust in His sickle on the earth, and the earth was reaped."

In the 21st century, the body of Christ now exists in a time like never before, because almost all of the entire world has been sowed to Jesus Christ. The world of today, knows an enormous amount of information about Him They just do not have what they know about Him, put together for themselves to understand why they need to accept Him as their Savior. Of course, there are many in remote places that are unreached and many in bondage to false religions throughout the world. We pray for them and try to reach them, but in America, Europe, Canada, Mexico, Central and South America, Australia, New Zealand, the Philippines and much of Africa, they have been sowed to Christ and are ready to be reaped. The unsaved throughout these nations have a massive amount of knowledge about Jesus Christ. These untold millions of unsaved people are ready to be reaped now, are willing to be reaped now and can be reaped now. For all who are evangelistically minded it is a simple matter getting equipped and moving from a sowing mindset into a reaping mindset. This can and will happen, once you learn the biblically strategized salvation gospel presentation and start leading unsaved family members, friends and strangers to accept Jesus Christ as their Savior.

WHY MOST PERSONAL EVANGELISM IS FOCUSED ON SOWING AND NOT REAPING

In personal evangelism the primary encouragements for decades, have been to "go witness, share your faith, share or give your testimony, build deep relationships or invite to church", which are all sowing processes. Most leaders do not expect many men, women or mature teens to actually lead an unsaved person to a decision to accept Jesus Christ as their Savior. At the same time, Christians, when they "witness", do not always expect to actually lead an unsaved person to an immediate decision for Christ. This is because "witnessing is non-specific." So, most hope that someone else will possibly lead them to Christ at a later time or under different circumstances. Church invitation is to invite unsaved people to attend, so perhaps another person may lead them to Christ. These basic personal evangelism scenarios are why I classify the traditional personal evangelism encouragements as sowing processes.

This strong sowing mindset is from the, well intended assumption, that if any person is unsaved, they must have and need to have Jesus Christ sowed into their lives. What is evangelistically overlooked is massive. It is the reality that, with the exception of those in remote or isolated areas, all unsaved people in the 21st century, already know a lot about Jesus Christ. They are already sowed to Christ and almost all are ready and willing to be reaped, which is to be led to their decision for Christ. Unsaved people today know a lot about Jesus Christ, but simply do not biblically understand what they have heard or know about Jesus Christ and they have all heard a lot about Him for most of their lives. This salvation gospel presentation puts it all together for them, which is why 95% to 100% of the time, when an unsaved person hears it, they are easily led to immediately pray to accept Jesus as their Savior.

The body of Christ declares "win the world to Christ or win your city or town to Christ", but with a go sow message, not a go reap message. This, in a nutshell, is why around 95% of the body of Christ has never led a single soul to a decision for Christ. This can all quickly change and be reversed after men, women and mature teens learn the biblically strategized salvation gospel presentation and learn what to say in order to be prepared to lead unsaved family members, friends or an occasional stranger to their decision to accept Jesus Christ as their Savior.

In the next chapter is the Biblically Strategized Salvation Gospel Presentation. As I introduced the personal evangelism goals, I stated that men, women and mature teens would be taught "what to say and why to say it, who to say it to, when to say it, where to say it and how to say it" in order to lead any unsaved person to accept Jesus Christ as their Savior. As you commit to continue through these next few chapters you will learn it all and will be prepared to lead any unsaved person to Christ.

> "To have the will to win is not what is important. It
> is the will to prepare to win that is important."
>
> Bobby Knight
> National Champion
> Basketball Coach

CHAPTER FIVE

THE BIBLICALLY STRATEGIZED SALVATION GOSPEL PRESENTATION

The biblically strategized salvation gospel presentation that you are about to learn will be very successful for you. It will, because it has the same personal evangelism subject matter and strategy that is in the bible. You are about to learn what to say and why to say it, who to say it to, when to say it, where to say it and how to say it. This is for you to know precisely what to say in order to introduce, present and conclude the salvation gospel with an immediate salvation result when you present it to unsaved family members, friends or an occasional stranger.

The biblical subject matter is physical death and spiritual death into salvation and a life in Christ. The strategy is to know what to say in order to gently, in a non-threatening way, introduce and present the coming death of an unsaved person. This is how to create an instant desire in an unsaved person to want to hear the salvation gospel of Jesus Christ. To then strategically transition into presenting the word of God in order to understandably explain about the danger from the coming death of all unsaved people and why all unsaved people need to receive Jesus as their Savior. Throughout the salvation gospel presentation, what to say is completely prepared for you. The structure and strategy of the salvation gospel presentation is in two parts. The bold print is for you to learn, memorize and gently present. It is separated by ongoing commentary, but keep in mind the bold print is to learn, memorize and present as one uninterrupted presentation. In other words, both parts are to be continuously presented as one part with no hesitation or pause. Always keep in mind that you will be successful when you present the biblically strategized salvation gospel presentation. This is because 95% to 100% of unsaved people that hear it, will immediately pray to receive Jesus as their Savior.

TWO STRATEGIC PARTS PRESENTED AS ONE

The first part is to create a teachable moment by preparing unsaved people to instantly want to hear the salvation gospel. This is done by bringing up the subject of death and to then strategically ask an unsaved person to give an answer about their own coming death. This is how the "teachable moment" is created, which duplicates exactly how Philip created a teachable moment in the Ethiopian eunuch. All unsaved people are uncertain about their coming death and want answers about their coming death. They will always give a "worldly" answer to the question about their own coming death. Then, there is a designed transitional statement to move past their response, no matter what it is, in order to uniquely present the word of God.

The second part is the actual presentation of the word of God that gives the biblical answers to any questions about the coming death of the unsaved person. This one of a kind salvation gospel presentation clearly and understandably explains the salvation gospel of Jesus Christ. When unsaved people hear the biblically strategized salvation gospel presentation, they completely understand why they need to immediately accept Jesus as their Savior. Its simple conclusion gently leads unsaved people through a prayer to receive Jesus as their Savior.

CHRISTIANS SHOULD ALWAYS BE IN CONTROL

This salvation gospel presentation has a very smooth and consistent flow from the moment you start it until you end it when the unsaved person prays to accept Jesus as Savior. This salvation gospel presentation was designed to give you, a witnessing Christian, the flexibility to take control of any conversation with an unsaved person. After you learn the biblically strategized salvation gospel presentation you will know what to say in order to change the subject of any conversation and introduce this uniquely designed salvation gospel presentation. Evangelism control simply means that you know what you are doing and know how to gently assert the direction of a conversation into this gospel presentation.

The biblically strategized salvation gospel presentation that you are about to learn should be presented like any normal conversation. This means to present it with a cool, calm and collected, almost passive tone in order for you to stay calm and keep an unsaved person calm. It is not an aggressive, loud or over the top intimidating salvation gospel presentation. It is a gently paced and uniquely strategized presentation of the salvation gospel of Jesus Christ. An example of being in control is whenever it is necessary, suggest and then lead an unsaved person to another location to avoid interruption.

WHEN IT IS TIME TO BEGIN

The appropriate time to begin is when the Holy Spirit or an Angel of the Lord, prompts, leads or gives you a sense that a particular person is available to hear the salvation gospel. When you feel led to start this strategized salvation gospel presentation, go ahead and begin with a calm and caring voice. For our training purposes we are going to use the name "Joe" for the unsaved person. This salvation gospel presentation is always presented the same way to a man, woman, boy or girl.

The bold print is for you to deeply memorize and present at the right time.

PART ONE: STATEMENTS, QUESTIONS AND TRANSITION

You and an unsaved person, who knows you are a Christian, could be doing anything or talking about anything. It will not matter if you are having a low-key witnessing conversation, talking about the weather or your favorite food. When you feel the Lord is prompting, impressing or leading you to lead the unsaved person to Christ, you simply begin the biblically strategized salvation gospel presentation by saying with a calm and sincere tone:

You Say: "Joe, as you know I'm a Christian and I do evangelism work, which means I talk to a lot of people about Jesus Christ, salvation and eternal life, things like that. May I ask you a question without being to personal?"

(they will normally give a quick "yes or ok", immediately keep going)

You Say: "You know we are all going to die someday, right?"

(Again, wait for their response, it's always "yes" Sometimes an unsaved person will look at you with a "deer in the headlight look". If they do, simply clarify by saying "I mean physically we are all going to die, right?" This statement will always bring them into reality and they always say "yes."

You say: "Let me ask you this Joe. When you die and it's time for you to go to heaven and Jesus Christ asks you 'Joe, why should I give you eternal life in heaven?' What would you say to Jesus?"

(Most of the time when this death and danger question is asked unsaved people will say: "I've tried to live a good life." They may say "I've tried to be a good person."

(This is their death and eternal danger question. "SAY NOTHING, STAY QUIET". They may blink or seem to struggle for a moment, but do not try to help them. The goal at this moment is for them to struggle. Let them answer on their own. It is a discovery question to find out what they know or think about Jesus Christ, eternal life and death issues. How they answer will reveal all you need to know about what they believe or think about Jesus Christ. Their answer is a vital step in their preparation to be led to Christ. This is how to bring an unsaved person to a "teachable moment.") THE RIGHT ANSWER IS "JESUS IS MY SAVIOR"

(At this moment, because of the impact of this unusual and deeply penetrating question, they might say anything. Most of the time their response, no matter who they are is quite predictable. Around 90% of the time their response will be something like "I've tried to be a good person, I've never hurt anyone or I've tried to live a good life." Generally, unsaved people promote themselves as responsible and view themselves as good and justify themselves as having good intentions. Since unsaved people only think of themselves as good, these kinds of answers are assumptive. They assume that since they think of themselves as people "trying to be a good person or live a good life" that they should deserve to go to heaven. Much of what unsaved people think or believe are from things "assumed." These responses are a classic example of Satan's temptation of Eve, when he told her in Gen 3:5 "For God knows that in the day you eat of it your eyes will be opened and you will be like God, knowing good and evil." Unsaved people make the assumption that if they have good intentions they deserve to go to heaven. They don't realize it, but they are making a God like judgement on why they should go to heaven. They are in essence their own Savior based on perceived good intentions and good works. Their responses are normally not deeply held, so expect them. As you will find, these type responses are quickly and easily brushed aside. No matter what they say do not challenge it. Always answer by saying "that's a normal response." Go immediately to the next step. Mirror back to them what they just said and put it in the context that what they just said is "a normal response." No matter what they say, it is normal to them and everyone likes to be told they are normal. This is being sensitive and accommodating and not confrontive in any way, shape, form or fashion.)

(As a result of this penetrating question an unsaved person could respond and say "I don't believe in heaven. I don't believe in Jesus, the bible, heaven or hell." The same principle applies, do not challenge them. Remember, they are not saved at this moment. The mission is to take them to the conclusion when they receive Christ, not to argue on the way. They are unsaved. This is why they do not believe in God, Jesus Christ, the bible, heaven or hell. They are at least, very confused about what they believe about these things. Again, do not challenge them or be distracted by their statements. Stay cool, calm and collected, keep going and do not think you have caught them in a "gotcha moment". The goal is to lead them to Christ, not confront them, correct them or put them down for saying something that is normal for an unsaved person. It does not matter what they say here, they are unsaved, keep going. Your response is "always the same" no matter what any unsaved person says in their response. This is all part of the preparation for them to hear the word of God.) This transition statement is designed to anticipate any response from an unsaved person. Therefore, you should always expect and anticipate that an unsaved person will give a wrong answer, but now you are prepared to easily handle it.

You Say: "That's a normal response, many people feel that way. I think most of us want to think we have tried to live a good life. Joe, let me share something with you that the bible says about that for you today."

(By you saying "that's a normal response" you have headed off any potential arguments. Most of the time unsaved people will respond with the "I've tried to be a good person, I've tried to live a good life" type answer. Occasionally, if someone does say that they don't "believe in God, Jesus, the bible, heaven or hell" and when they do say that, they may be expecting to be confronted and may be expecting an argument. Don't give them one or confront them. Tell them, even if they say the things that "don't make sense" or something you know that they probably don't deeply believe in, "That's a normal response. Some people don't believe in God, Jesus Christ, the bible, heaven or hell. Joe, let me share something with you that the bible says about that for you, today."

(No matter what they say it is always "a normal response" in order to transition and go on to the next step, which is the presentation of the three scriptures. All unsaved people like to hear that whatever they said "is normal." It is a comforting and calming statement for them to hear. This is a transitional response statement on your part that will satisfy an unsaved person and allow you to maintain control of the gospel presentation flow. The entire introductory statements process and eternal danger question is to bring an unsaved person to the position of wanting to instantly hear the word of God presented to them. The unsaved person has been brought to a teachable moment and they are ready to be taught through this gospel presentation.)

(Through the strategic statements and questions that you just presented, you have led an unsaved person to a place of danger and vulnerability. You created their teachable moment and now you will lead them through these three short scriptures to reveal to them the real extent of their eternal danger. At the conclusion of presenting and explain these three scriptures, you will lead them into eternal safety by receiving Jesus Christ as their Savior.)

As you present these three scriptures, present and explain them as if they are one. Do not hesitate or pause between the scriptures. Most importantly, "never slow down or stop to ask any unsaved person if they understand what you are presenting or if they have any questions about what you are presenting." They know and understand exactly what you are telling them. Keep this in mind. It is dangerous if you pause or ask them if they have questions or understand what you are presenting. It is dangerous, because you can lose control of the presentation by letting them talk about irrelevant things and take the conversation in a completely wrong direction. If they interrupt, simply tell them you will answer them at the end. (Continue into part two as one continuous flow of presentation.)

PART TWO: THREE SCRIPTURES, AN INVITATION AND CONCLUDING PRAYER

You say: "Joe, the bible has two sections, the old testament and the new testament. In the new testament in Romans 3:23, the bible says, 'For all have sinned and come short of the glory of God.' Joe, that is a reference back to when Adam and Eve were in the Garden of Eden. God told them that they could have dominion over everything in the garden. Just don't do one thing, don't eat of the fruit of the tree of the knowledge of good and evil, or they would surely die. That's the old apple story. Adam and Eve ate of the fruit and that act of disobedience brought sin into the world and separated mankind from God spiritually for all eternity. Joe, when the bible talks about death, unless it refers to a specific physical death, it is talking about spiritual death. Joe, as a result of that original sin in the Garden of Eden, we are all born spiritually separated from God."

(Everyone is familiar with the Adam and Eve story and when you include the reference to the "old apple story", they always smile and nod in agreement. They are with you 100%!)

You say: "Joe in Romans 6:23, the bible says 'For the wages of sin is death.' Joe, just like we receive wages for the work that we do, because of that original sin, we receive the wages of a spiritual death. Joe, people that are living and don't know God in their heart know that they really do not know God. When they die, because they didn't know God in this life, they won't know God in eternal life. This is when the issue of heaven and hell comes up.

Joe, the second half of that scripture says 'but the gift of God is eternal life through Jesus Christ our Lord.' What that means is that when Jesus was here on the earth, He went to the cross and took upon Himself the sin of the world. He died, was buried and on the third day, He arose from the dead and later ascended to heaven. Joe, if we accept Jesus' sacrifice on the cross for our sins, repent of our sins and ask forgiveness for our sins, our sins are forgiven and when we die, we can have eternal life in heaven."

You continue and say: "Joe, in Romans 10:9, the bible says, 'If you confess with your mouth the Lord Jesus and believe in your heart that God has raised Him from the dead, you will be saved.' Joe, when the bible talks about being saved, it means you must be saved from something; you are saved from going to hell and saved from living this life separated from God. Let me ask you this Joe, would you like to know that you can have eternal life in heaven someday?"

(Wait for their answer. It will come quickly and it will be yes.) When they say: Yes, immediately go to this next step with no pause or hesitation.

You say: "Okay Joe, I'd like to lead you in a short prayer for you to accept Jesus Christ as your Savior, then repent and ask forgiveness for your sins. When you pray, your sins are all forgiven and when you die, you will have eternal life in heaven. I will lead the prayer, you repeat the prayer. Will you pray with me?"

Again, when they say: yes

You say: "Joe, this is your prayer, I will lead the prayer, you repeat the prayer: "Heavenly Father, I accept Jesus Christ as my Savior. I repent of my sins, I ask you to forgive me of my sins, give me eternal life in heaven and I will seek your will for my life. In Jesus' name I pray, Amen. (As soon as the unsaved person has finished praying to receive Jesus as their Savior, immediately affirm their decision. Affirm their decision and give some basic direction on what they should do next upon receiving Jesus as Savior. The following are optional suggestions. You can use any or all of the following or add as you feel you should say to them. Keep in mind that leading an unsaved person to Christ can take place anywhere and anytime. Encourage them as best you can.)

You say: "May God bless you and never forget this date. On this date you confessed Jesus as your Savior by praying to receive Him as your Savior, which is the answer to the (when you die and it's time to go to heaven) question. To repent of sin is to go in a new direction in Jesus Christ by having faith in Him and to seek His will for your life. Your sins are now forgiven, you are now right with God and you will have eternal life in heaven. In the future if and when you sin, repent of your sin, ask Him to forgive you and He will. He does not give license to sin. He is the only way to live forgiven and free from the grip of sin. The bible teaches the next step is to find a bible believing church to learn more about Him and grow more deeply in Him. I suggest......". (At this point pray for any needs they have and invite them to your own church, suggest another or explain to them the need to find a solid bible believing church)

THAT'S IT YOU JUST LED JOE TO THE LORD

Leading an unsaved person to Christ, irrespective, if is a family member, friend or stranger, will take place exactly as this "real life model" of the biblically strategized salvation gospel presentation just demonstrated. However, when you feel the Lord is prompting, impressing or leading you to lead a stranger to Christ, simply approach them and with a calm sincere tone: **You Say: Hello, my name is _____,I'm a Christian and I do evangelism work, which means I talk to a lot of people about Jesus Christ, salvation and eternal life, things like that. May**

I ask you a question without being to personal?".....and just continue the presentation. It doesn't take long. The impact of the word of God upon a prepared and receptive unsaved person is powerful and life changing. You, a witnessing Christian prepared them to instantly want to hear and then be ready to receive the word of God. You then very clearly presented the word of God and the power in the word of God will eliminate any thought or hesitation to receive Christ. To accept and receive Jesus Christ as Savior is a step of faith. This uniquely strategized salvation gospel presentation is to present the word of God to an unsaved person, in order to create faith in an unsaved person.

Hebrews 4:12, "For the Word of God is quick, and powerful, and sharper than any twoedged sword, piercing even to the dividing asunder of soul and spirit, and of the joints and marrow, and is a discerner of the thoughts and intents of the heart."

Isaiah 55:11, "So shall my word be that goes forth from My mouth. It shall not return to me void, but it shall accomplish what I please, And shall prosper in the thing for which I sent it."

Romans 10:17, "So then faith comes by hearing and hearing by the Word of God."

2 Timothy 3:16, "All scripture is given by inspiration of God, and is profitable for doctrine, for reproof, for correction, for instruction in righteousness, that the man of God may be complete, thoroughly equipped for every good work." (If an unsaved person does not pray to accept Jesus as their Savior, they may say something like "I think I'm good for now, I think I'm alright for now" or some variation of those themes.) If they do, **You Say: "I understand. Joe, some people think that if they are a good person, don't hurt people and want to help people they will get to go to heaven. Joe, they could help ten little old ladies cross a street every day, but none of those are why people go to heaven. Joe, we were all created in the image of God to be spiritual and spirit led people of God. As a result of original sin in the Garden of Eden, our spirit is not alive when we are physically born and we are**

then born spiritually separated from God. When we accept to receive Jesus as our Savior, ours sins are forgiven, we are right with God and our spirt comes to life. This is what born again means and why Jesus said you must be born again to see the kingdom of God. Jn 3:3 "Jesus answered and said to him, "Most assuredly, I say to you, unless one is born again, he cannot see the kingdom of God." This and then living righteously is the only reason anyone can go to heaven. Let me lead you in a prayer for you to receive Jesus as your Savior."(If they say no) **You Say: "I understand. When you are alone don't forget what we talked about. You can pray on your own and ask Jesus to be your Savior. Jesus loves you and may God bless you."**

THE MOST POWERFUL WORDS AN UNSAVED PERSON CAN HEAR ARE THE WORDS OF GOD

These glorious scriptures establish that presenting and interpreting the Word of God is the most powerful way to communicate the salvation gospel of Jesus Christ. He separates His words from ours by letting us know that just by hearing His word, something powerful and glorious will take place in the soul of the one who hears it. An unsaved person can forget or brush aside your words or mine, but the Word of God has power beyond anything that Christians can really grasp or understand except by faith. Keep in mind that all unsaved people already know a lot about Jesus Christ and have good feelings about Him. You prepared them to want to hear the word of God and clearly explained to them as you presented the word of God, exactly why any unsaved person needs to accept Jesus as their Savior. The word of God is powerful and unsaved people are touched and moved by the power in His word.

YOUR WORDS OR MINE HAVE NO POWER

Experts in communication believe the human spoken word accounts for only 7% of what whatever is communicated. They say 55% is tone, 35% is body language and 3% is location. I am communicating with words that you understand. The word of God communicates with His anointed words that an unsaved person will understand. This is why it is so critically important in personal evangelism to focus on presenting His word, not ours. This is exactly what this strategized salvation gospel does and will do for you. This is the "Art and Skill" of leading unsaved people to Christ. The skill is to know what to say, which is what the biblically strategized salvation gospel presentation will give you. The art is to just be yourself, being cool, calm and collected with a kind and gentle tone as you present the biblically strategized salvation gospel presentation.

GENERALLY UNSAVED PEOPLE RESPOND ALIKE

Most unsaved people will respond to the death and danger question with predictable statements. The most common are "I've tried to live a good life, be a good person or never hurt anyone" or variations of these same ideas. Some may say "That's a hard question, a good question or that's a difficult or interesting question." Some may simply say "I don't know" No matter what they say, your response is always the same: "THAT'S A NORMAL RESPONSE". Keep in mind that they are responding to your penetrating question about what they would say to Jesus. Patiently listen to them, their answers come quickly, but you will be prepared for whatever they say back to you. You will be prepared when you memorize and learn the strategized salvation gospel presentation. If you have ever heard the expression "ordinary people doing extraordinary things", that expression will certainly apply to whomever learns the biblically strategized salvation gospel presentation and starts winning souls.

From time to time a few unsaved people may respond to the death and danger question by saying: "I believe there are many ways to God. All religions lead to God." If an unsaved person answers that way; **You Say: "That's a normal response. I know some people believe that way. Let me share something with you that the bible says about that for you today. In the new testament in John 4:16, Jesus Christ Himself states "I am the way, the truth, and the life. No one comes to the Father except through Me." "Joe, the truth is there is only one way to God and eternal life in heaven and that is by receiving Jesus as your Savior, having your sins forgiven and then have eternal life in heaven." In Rom 3:23 the bible says.....**

An unsaved person may respond to the death and danger question and say "I believe the universe will take care of things or I believe in Astrology." If an unsaved person answers that way: **You Say: "That's a normal response. I know some people believe that way. Let me share something with you that the bible says about that for you today." "Joe, in the old testament, in the very first verse in Genesis 1:1 the bible says "In the beginning God created the heavens and the earth." Joe, we are all to worship the Creator, not the created. When people trust in the universe or Astrology they are actually trusting in the created and not the Creator" In Rom 3:23 the bible says......**

Some unsaved people may respond to the death and danger question and say: "I believe the bible was written by people that made up stories and fairy tales." If an unsaved person answers that way: **You Say: "That's a normal response. I know some people believe that way. Let me share something with you that the bible says about that for you today." "Joe, in the** new testament in 2Timothy3:16a the bible says "All scripture is given by inspiration of God" "Joe, this means that God inspired and led the people who wrote the bible to write it as He and He alone wanted it to be written. The word of God is truth and we can completely have faith in it and that the people who wrote it were led of Him." In Rom 3:23 the bible says.........

If and when unsaved people give these kinds of answers to the death and danger question, then adjust with the clarifying statements, include the appropriate scriptures where you feel led to do so and then go to Rom: 3:23 and continue through the biblically strategized salvation gospel presentation.

THE BIBLICALLY STRATEGIZED SALVATION GOSPEL PRESENTATION STAYS WITH THEM

Although it is rare, if an unsaved person for whatever reason does not receive Jesus as Savior after he or she hears the biblically strategized salvation gospel presentation, there is still a powerful result. The result is the unsaved person has heard a prepared and powerful presentation of the word of God in this salvation gospel presentation, including the eternal need to receive Jesus as Savior. The Lord wanted the unsaved person to hear this penetrating salvation gospel presentation to know why they need to receive Jesus as their Savior. They then know what to pray on their own to receive Jesus as Savior. This is in opposition to unsaved people hearing generalized, unstructured witnessing, which many times is not understandable, because it could be about anything that relates to God, Jesus, the bible, heaven, hell, church, or the personal experience of a Christian. As you will learn, this is why the bible demonstrates and calls for Christians to be prepared to present Christ with a biblically strategized salvation gospel presentation.

A MAN HEARD THE SALVATION GOSPEL PRESENTATION SAID HE COULDN'T ACCEPT JESUS BUT SOON DID

I presented the strategized salvation gospel presentation to a man that I had just met. He happened to be an attorney. He said that he would like to accept Jesus as his Savior, but could not. He explained that he was a gentile and his wife was Jewish with three children and their life revolved around her family. A few weeks later he approached me and told me that on his own, he prayed to accept Jesus as his Savior and was now praying for his wife children.

When the strategized salvation gospel presentation is presented to an unsaved person it is rare if any unsaved person does not immediately accept Jesus Christ as their Savior.

An unsaved person clearly heard the word of God, pray for them that they will pray on their own. You were led to present the salvation gospel to them and they heard it. The Holy Spirt knows something about them that you may never know and do not need to know. Heb 4:12 "For the word of God is living and powerful, and sharper than any two-edged sword, piercing even to the division of soul and spirt, and of joints and marrow, and is a discerner of the thoughts and intents of the heart." His word will not fail.

CHAPTER SIX

ANALYSIS OF THE BIBLICALLY STRATEGIZED SALVATION GOSPEL PRESENTATION

The function of part #1 is to prepare and instantly create immediate vulnerability about the coming death of an unsaved person and to create a teachable moment for them to want to hear answers about their coming death. The strategy of introducing death and the unique question about the coming death of an unsaved person is that it will create an instant desire for an unsaved person to want to hear the answer to their coming death. It is also to discover what an unsaved person thinks, knows or understands about Jesus Christ and eternal death issues. In "general or vague" witnessing interactions between Christians and unsaved people, unsaved people guard what they truly believe.

The death and danger question will draw out a response from them, that they basically know is not the right answer. Unsaved people are never prepared to deal with the penetrating question "Let me ask you this. When you die and it's time for you to go to Heaven and Jesus Christ asks you, why should I give you eternal life in heaven, what would you say to Jesus?" Unsaved people are never ready for this unusually designed question about their own death. They may be used to discussing the death of others, but never their own coming death.

A UNIQUELY DESIGNED QUESTION ABOUT COMING DEATH

The death and danger question is the immediate follow up question to the harmless agreeing statement of "We are all going to die someday, right?" An unsaved person is expecting another harmless type question from you, but that is not what takes place. The death and danger question, has a very harmless sounding introduction "Let me ask you this Joe." It sounds as if you are going to ask another harmless and simple question, but the question is strategically shifted to become a question as if it is from Jesus Christ Himself. Suddenly, the unsaved person has been placed in the position of now being asked to explain what they would say to Jesus Christ that would justify why He should give them eternal life in heaven.

UNSAVED PEOPLE WILL BE VULNERABLE
AND SHAKEN TO THE CORE

They may not show it, but they are unprepared and are shaken to the core with this deep and powerful question. This is a penetrating question for an unsaved person to deal with, they always give their self promoting answer. They will then absolutely want to hear the correct answer from you. All unsaved people are extremely teachable at this moment. At times an unsaved person will answer the "death and danger" by saying "that's a hard question." When they do, simply say "that's a normal response, many people think this is a hard question. Let me share something with you that the bible says about that for you, today." Then continue the salvation gospel presentation.

THE ANSWERS FROM UNSAVED PEOPLE
ARE WEAK AND SELF PROMOTING

It is amazing and quite predictable how most of the answers from unsaved people to the death and danger question are very similar and almost identical. The most common are almost always a variation of "I've tried to be a good person or I've tried to live a good life and I've never hurt anyone" These are answers to justify why the Lord should let them into heaven. In the mind of unsaved people, it is only "bad people" that die and go to hell. These same unsaved people never think of themselves as "bad people." This is why they think their idealistic "good works attitude" of trying to be a good person, or living a good life and never hurting anyone, will get them to heaven. To the unsaved, salvation is based upon "works."

UNSAVED PEOPLE ARE ABOUT TO BE TOLD THE TRUTH

Answers from unsaved people to the "death and danger" question are almost always virtuous sounding and self-promoting type answers. In other words, because they "tried to be a good person or tried to live a good life and never hurt anyone" they deserve to get to go to heaven. When they answer like this, it is clear that they are unsaved. You have discovered what they do not know about death and eternal life. They are discovering that they do not know the right answer, which is that Jesus Christ is the Savior. They know deep down, that they probably do not have the right answer and that you do have the right answer. They know that you know, that they do not know the right answer and they will want to hear the right answer from you.

HOW THIS ONE OF A KIND STRATEGY WORKS

1. The opening and introduction statement to directly start or shift from one conversation into the beginning of the gospel presentation. When you say "I talk to a lot of people about Jesus Christ, salvation and eternal life, things like that." It is a vague reference to death. This is a simple statement of the reality that you have talked about these things with people. It gives you credibility,

because you are stating that you talk to a lot of people about these subjects. The implication is that you know what you are talking about. Irrespective of when, where or to whom you talked with about these issues. The truth is, you have talked to people about Jesus Christ, salvation and eternal life.

2. When you ask, "May I ask you a question without being to personal?" They will say "yes." You then ask, "You know we are all going to die someday, right?" This is a general reference to death. This is another simple, disarming and very polite way to ask permission to continue the conversation. They know a question is coming, but have no idea what is about to be asked of them. When they say, "yes", they are responding to you, which means you have led them into the strategized salvation gospel presentation.

You now have them exactly where you want them. The rest of the strategized gospel presentation is simply leading an unsaved person through the death and danger question, the transition statement to present the word of God, concluding by leading them to receive Jesus as Savior in the prayer. You are in control and will maintain control by keeping the gospel presentation moving. To say you have led them into the presentation, is another way of saying you have "caught" them. Jesus told Peter and Andrew that they would become fishers of men. He meant that for the entire body of Christ and this is how to catch them. This simple question is your bait and when they bite, the rest of this gospel presentation reels them in to hearing the salvation gospel and receiving Jesus as Savior.

Matt 4:18-19 "And Jesus walking by the sea of Galilee, saw two brothers, Simon called Peter, and Andrew his brother, casting a net into the sea; for they were fishermen. Then He said to them, "Follow Me, and I will make you fishers of men."

3. When you ask the death and danger question "Let me ask you this Joe, when you die and it's time for you to go to heaven and Jesus Christ asks you, 'Joe, why should I give you eternal life in heaven.?' What would you say to Jesus?" This is a direct reference to the coming death of the unsaved person. They have been prepared to hear about death, with a vague reference to death, a general reference to death and now a direct, very penetrating reference to their own coming death. They have been awakened to the reality that they are suddenly in the midst of a very serious conversation about their own future death and eternity. Keep in mind, you are the one who knows what is happening and coming next, they have no idea what is coming next. They are being led, because you are leading them. You have led them to a teachable moment. A large part of the teachable moment is you have "drawn out of them or caused them" to express and reveal what they think about their own coming death and eternal life. They want to know the right answer about death and eternal life. You led them to "open up" about something they know nothing about and in doing so, prepared them to want you to give them the right answer.

4. Unsaved people always respond to the "Death and Danger" question. The next step is for you to respond to whatever their response is and transition them past their response in order to begin to present the word of God with the designed conclusion.

EVERYONE ACCEPTS THE REALITY
THAT SOMEDAY THEY WILL DIE

Your gentle authority, control and trust is established, because of the sensitive way you are handling the subject of death and the coming death of the unsaved person. When you directly bring up the coming death on an unsaved person with a "when you die and it is time for you to go to heaven" question, it is both a realistic and credible question. The question context is realistic and credible and therefore, so are you. Everyone expects to die in the future. All people understand that death can possibly come at any moment, but no one seriously expects it. This is why the death and danger question is framed on a "when you die" basis, and not on a "if you die today or tonight" basis. Everything in this strategized gospel presentation is designed to sound sincere, normal, credible and realistic. As a result, unsaved people always feel secure and safe at all times when you present this gospel presentation to them.

DEEP DOWN UNSAVED PEOPLE KNOW
WHAT THEY REALLY DON'T KNOW

Unsaved people immediately realize that they probably do not have a good or right answer. This is primarily because an unsaved person's biblical and theological understanding about death is close to zero. Keep in mind, it's a response based on an unsaved person's idealized mindset. This mindset is that "just being a good person, trying to be a good person or not wanting to hurt anyone" is the way to heaven. At this moment they will want to hear from you. They all absolutely want the right answer. Metaphorically, you "have them on the edge of their seat." As soon as they give their answer, no matter what it is, tell them that their response is "normal", never confront their answer, but always make the transitional statement.

THE TRANSITIONAL STATEMENT WAS DESIGNED
TO ANTICIPATE ANY KIND OF RESPONSE

The transitional statement or bridge statement serves a very specific purpose. It was designed to anticipate any possible response that an unsaved person has to the death and danger question. It was designed to give you, a witnessing Christian, a mechanism to avoid dealing with directly or answering inaccurate responses that would lead to unnecessary and extended conversations about whatever was just stated. The strategy of the "that's a normal response" transitional statement is to gently and diplomatically brush their response aside in order to for you to present the word of God.

THE TRANSITION TELLS THE UNSAVED THAT THE BIBLE HAS SOMETHING FOR THEM

The strategy is to quickly, yet sensitively, move past whatever their response might be to the "death and danger question." You, a credible witnessing Christian, are telling them that the bible has something to say about what they just stated and it is about them. This is a huge and intriguing statement to an unsaved person. They always want to hear everything you want to tell them. This is because of the sensitive way you transitioned into preparing them to hear the word of God. You did not insult or offend them, but sensitively transitioned into what you want to do, which is to present the salvation gospel of Jesus Christ

YOU KNOW WHAT IS COMING NEXT WITH THIS GOSPEL PRESENTATION

The transitional statement was designed for Christians to move past whatever an unsaved person states in their response to the death and danger question. It is a strategic transition to allow you to immediately begin presenting the salvation gospel of Jesus Christ. The transitional statement moves both you and the unsaved person into the word of God. It is now you presenting the word of God to a prepared unsaved person that wants to hear the word of God and at the conclusion, will immediately accept and receive Jesus as their Savior. You always know what is coming next with the biblically strategized salvation gospel presentation.

NOT A "GOTCHA MOMENT"

An unsaved person may expect an immediate corrective statement, don't give them one, don't correct them, but transition them. The death and danger question is not to trap unsaved people in order to put them down in an "I gotcha way." They are unsure and vulnerable here and do not know what is going on or coming next. The unsaved person knows that they have suddenly revealed something about what they think or believe that they would not have ordinarily revealed. They have been led into a deep question about what they think, know or understand about their own coming death and they all want to know the truth and the right answer.

THEY RESPECT AND APPRECIATE THE GENTLE
WAY YOU ARE HANDLING THEM

Every unsaved person will respect and appreciate how you are handling a very sensitive and serious subject. They realize that in the midst of this "to them a religious conversation", they are being talked to and handled in a very polite and courteous way. Again, maintain a cool, calm and collected composure through this process. You know what you are doing, where this salvation gospel presentation is going to go, so stay cool, calm and collected. The statement in the transition statement about the bible having something that relates to them is exciting, encouraging and comforting. When you say, "That's a normal response Joe, let me share something with you that the bible says about that for you today", to an unsaved person, they are ready and want to hear what you are going to tell them.

"THAT'S A NORMAL RESPONSE" IS STRATEGIC
NOT A STATEMENT OF AGREEMENT

When you, a witnessing Christian, say "that's a normal response" you are not agreeing with whatever they just said, but are acknowledging and affirming their right to say whatever they just said. When you give them the transitional statement, you are simply telling them their response is normal so treat it as normal. Do not smirk, smile, giggle, groan, have a shocked look on your face or roll your eyes. Some answers will sound humorous. One young man answered the death and danger question about why Jesus should give him eternal life in heaven, by saying "because my uncle was a church deacon!" I calmly told him, "That's a normal response. I can tell you came from a good family. Let me share something with you that the bible says about that for you today." At the conclusion of the strategized salvation gospel presentation he prayed to receive Jesus as his Savior.

NO MATTER HOW THEY RESPOND IT IS
ALWAYS "THAT'S A NORMAL RESPONSE"

When witnessing Christians learn this gospel presentation, they will always know what to do and say to an unsaved person. If you are presenting the gospel presentation and an unsaved person responds to the "death and danger" question by including something like "all people in church are hypocrites." Tell them "that's a normal response, I know some people think that churches are full of hypocrites and there are probably a few, but let me share something with you that the bible says about that for you today." Keep in mind that the statement "that's a normal response" is a strategic statement that is designed for virtually any response to the "death and danger" question. Always use it in a sensitive and calm way and it will smooth the way for you to present the salvation gospel of Jesus Christ with a salvation result.

STAY COOL CALM AND COLLECTED AND LET THE STRUCTURE AND STRATEGY WORK

This is a structured and strategized salvation gospel presentation, so let the structure and strategy work for both you and the unsaved person. This is a tender moment about a tender subject and this gentle transition opens the door for you to present truths and answers that are only found in the word of God. At this point, they will follow you with great desire and interest in what you have to tell them. It is important to not appear excited or anxious. Continue to maintain a cool, calm and collected composure. If you are calm, they will be calm. If you are nervous, they will be nervous. Once you start this gospel presentation there is no reason to ever be nervous. Everything that happens, including an unsaved person receiving Jesus as their Savior, is completely predictable, so trust the Lord, trust this strategized salvation gospel presentation and the power in this gospel presentation will do the work for you.

Proverbs 15:1-2 "A soft word turns away wrath, but a harsh word stirs up anger. The tongue of the wise uses knowledge rightly, but the mouths of fools pours for foolishness.

THE BIBLICALLY STRATEGIZED SALVATION GOSPEL PRESENTATION KEEPS YOU AND THE UNSAVED FOCUSED

This unique gospel presentation keeps you focused and on task. It gives both you and an unsaved person a calm and smooth structure to prevent either of you from getting argumentative or emotionally upset. It also eliminates getting sidetracked and off the subject at hand. The gospel presentation will prevent you from forgetting things that you want to say or present to an unsaved person. Have you ever walked away from a witnessing conversation with an unsaved person and thought "I wish I had remembered to say this or that?" When you learn this gospel presentation, everything you need to know in order to lead or win an unsaved person to Christ is in it.

IF YOU ARE WITH AN UNSAVED PERSON THAT IS ABOUT TO DIE

This can sound challenging and uncomfortable, but do not fear. If you are with an unsaved person that is about to die, they know that they are near death. When you are with them, they have probably already been told by a medical person or family member. Pray for the strength of the Lord and He will be with you and the dying unsaved person. Gently start the biblically strategized salvation gospel presentation and slowly talk it to them. They will understand, will welcome this message and will receive Jesus as their Savior. Years ago, a lady from my former church asked me to visit a friend from her work and lead him to Christ. He was a young man in the hospital dying from Aids. I went and his Mother met me at the door.

At first, she was hesitant to let me in, because her son's "partner" was there with three of their friends. She knew I was there specifically to lead her son to a decision for Christ and wanted me to lead her son to Christ. She was a Christian, but was confused and conflicted in the moment by her son's coming death and the unexpected presence of her son's "partner." She had a moment of confusion about me coming in, since her son's "partner" was in the room. I told her that I understood, but I was not there to deal with any "politically correct" relational issues, but to lead her son to his salvation in Jesus Christ. This direct statement to her snapped her out of her confusion and she then quickly let me in and we went directly to his bedside.

NO MATTER THE CIRCUMSTANCES OR WHO YOU ARE WITH ALWAYS BE GENTLE AND SLOW

I slowly and with a gentle tone talked the biblically strategized salvation gospel presentation to him. The young man was so weak that he could not speak above an unintelligible whisper. I instructed him to hold his mother's hand and as I was leading him to accept Jesus as his Savior, that he would squeeze her hand to let she and I know that he was accepting Jesus as his Savior as he prayed to accept Christ. As I led him in what to pray, with tears in his eyes, he squeezed her hand to acknowledge that he was accepting Jesus as his Savior. He accepted and received Jesus as his Savior. After I led the young man to his decision to receive Jesus as his Savior, I attempted to speak with the others in the room. Even though I spoke gently to the young man, I knew the others in the room could hear everything I said to him. The "partner" was upset, did not understand what just took place and did not want me to explain what just took place. I left the hospital room and the young man died before dawn.

BE PREPARED TO IMMEDIATELY LEAD OR WIN AN UNSAVED PERSON TO JESUS CHRIST

If you are with an unsaved person about to die there is no time to pause, hesitate or wait. This is not the time for sensitive general witnessing, general faith sharing or personal testimony. This is the moment and time to lead a dying man or woman to immediately accept Jesus Christ as their Savior. With the biblically strategized salvation gospel presentation you will know exactly what to say and do to instantly lead or win a dying unsaved person to receive Jesus Christ as their Savior. Keep in mind that all unsaved people are in the same condition. I just happened to be with this young man in the final moments of his life. All unsaved people will come to the final hours of their lives still unsaved, unless a man, woman or mature teen leads them to Jesus Christ as their Savior.

CHAPTER SEVEN

PREPARED BY YOU TO WANT TO
RECEIVE JESUS AS THEIR SAVIOR

In section #1, you have prepared an unsaved person to be extremely interested in hearing what the bible has to say about their own coming death. The teachable moment and transition statement process has opened the door for you to now present the word of God. The #2 part of the salvation gospel presentation is for you to now present the word of God with an understandable explanation, which concludes by leading them to accept Jesus as their Savior. Keep in mind that you are probably not the first person that has tried to explain something "religious" to an unsaved person. They may have encountered "Mormons, Jehovah Witnesses, Buddhists, Scientologists or other well intentioned, but unprepared Christians." You are going to present the word of God through the biblically strategized salvation gospel presentation in a way that they have never heard so understandably clear.

YOU LED THEM TO DANGER NOW LEAD THEM TO SAFETY

Now is the time to lead the unsaved person to their salvation in Jesus Christ and to safety. You led them to danger with the death and danger question, by asking them to give an answer about how they would answer for their death and danger. You have led them to a place of personal jeopardy, vulnerability and danger. The presentation of the word of God in this gospel presentation will explain and clarify why the only hope to have salvation, safety and eternal life in heaven is through Jesus Christ. You led them to danger, you now lead them out of danger and into salvation and safety by leading them as they accept and receive Jesus as Savior.

ALL OF HUMANITY IS IN THE SAME SITUATION

The initial value of presenting and explaining Romans 3:23 is that unsaved people will hear and understand that original sin is the problem for all of humanity. It explains the sin condition and position of unsaved people in a gentle way that is easily comprehended and understood. This helps to begin to move an unsaved person out of and away from only seeing others as "bad, because they did bad things" as deserving of hell. It will teach them that everyone is in the same situation as a result of what theologians generally refer to as "original sin or the fall of man." The unsaved person is beginning to go through a transformative view of their perception of sin and who is a sinner. They are beginning to understand that not just "bad criminals or perceived bad people" are in sin. You are bringing them to a place where for the first time, they are beginning to realize that they themselves have a sin problem.

DON'T UNDERESTIMATE CHILDREN SO PRESENT
THIS SALVATION GOSPEL TO THEM

When presenting this salvation gospel to a child, do so calmly and gently. They will completely understand what they are hearing from you. Romans 3:23, is focused on sin. After saying, "For all have sinned and come short of the glory of God" simply interject that "sin is what causes people to do the things, that they know they should not do." This simple statement is one that even younger children completely understand. Many feel they should not try and lead a young child to Christ for fear that they would not understand what they are doing. Children do not understand everything, but they know they accepted Jesus as their Savior. They can and will learn about the things of God as they are taken to a bible believing church with a Sunday School Program for children.

A POWERFUL SCRIPTURE THAT HAS
THE PROBLEM AND SOLUTION

Romans 6:23 is a very unique scripture. It is unique, because it has both the problem of being unsaved and solution of receiving Jesus as Savior, built into it. In other words, it has both the problem and solution in this one short text. The first part is the recognition of the problem and the result of the problem. The second part is the gift of God that is the solution and only solution to the sin problem. The solution is eternal life through Jesus Christ.

Romans 6:23 "For the wages of sin is death, but the gift of God is eternal life through Jesus Christ our Lord."

EVERYONE UNDERSTANDS WAGES

Everyone understands what receiving wages means from the work that they do. Even homeless people completely understand this point. They are also hearing more about death. The wages of sin are clearly explained and related to original sin and spiritual death in a way that all unsaved people understand and they all "get it." You, the witnessing Christian, are making a very powerful statement. "People who are living that don't know God, in their hearts, know that they don't really know God." In a tactful and subtle way, you are telling them that it is they who do not know God. By the framing of the statement and the gentleness of your presentation, the unsaved person knows that this statement is about him or her. You know it is about them and they know that you know that it is about them. A subtle hand gesture towards their heart, like pointing towards them, just helps with the unspoken confirmation that, yes, it is about them.

THE BAD NEWS AND THE EXPLANATION
OF THE ULTIMATE PROBLEM

When an unsaved person hears, "When they die, because he or she didn't know God in this life, he or she won't know God in eternal life. This is when the issue of heaven or hell comes up." The unsaved person knows that the reference to the person that dies is him or her. You have been raising the issue of their death and the unsaved person also knows that they do not know God. They are now hearing about a frightening reality that is gently being explained to them. Unsaved people already know about heaven and hell, but you are explaining hell to them with a new, uncomplicated and understandable explanation.

UNSAVED PEOPLE WON'T MISS IT THEY ALL GET IT

They all get the point about hell. This gospel presentation presents a simple reality of hell in a way that the unsaved person can easily grasp for their own life and death situation. Hell is introduced in a gentle and almost casual way. It will not sound like you a witnessing Christian are "browbeating them, are trying to scare them or lecture them" about the danger of hell.

UNSAVED PEOPLE REALIZE WHAT THEY
THOUGHT WAS TRUE IS NOT TRUE

This is not random, directionless, general or vague witnessing. It is focused, intentional, very clear and unsaved people are receiving a brief, but very solid biblical education. They are hearing and realizing that the potential to go to hell is not just for bad people from a preconceived notion that certain serious criminal types are those who go to hell. Unsaved people realize that what they thought was true, is actually not true. They are discovering that separation from God now and in eternity is not from "bad acts by bad people", but from original sin in the garden of Eden.

NOW THE SOLUTION AND SAFETY

After the bad news, the good news that the unsaved person has been prepared to hear and now ready to receive, is about to be presented. They have been told about the danger of hell and they realize that they are vulnerable and know they are in great danger. They are about to hear the solution that Jesus Christ is the only hope for them. In just a few moments they will turn to Him for their own salvation and safety.

Romans 6:23b "but the gift of God is eternal life through Jesus Christ our Lord."

In Romans 6:23b, the focus is on receiving the gift of God from what Jesus Christ did on the cross. Unsaved people now understand that Jesus took upon Himself the sin of the world, which includes their own sins. They now understand that He died for the sins of everyone. If anyone accepts Jesus, repents of their sins, asks forgiveness for their sins, their sins are forgiven. The gift is when they die, they can go to heaven. The focus here is on "we" as in what Jesus did on the cross was for everyone. It includes what "we" as in everyone" can do in response to His work on the cross. This prepares them to understand Romans 10:9 where the focus turns to "you" the unsaved and the conclusion of them being led to their immediate decision to receive Jesus Christ as their Savior.

THEY ARE READY TO RECEIVE JESUS BECAUSE
YOU PREPARED AND LED THEM

The unsaved person has been gently confronted in a sensitive and tactful way about their coming death and the eternal blessing of what choosing Jesus as Savior can mean to anyone who accepts Him. At this moment they are hearing from the word of God how they can miss hell and that is good news for every unsaved person to hear. This far along in the gospel presentation unsaved people are already mentally and emotionally choosing to make their decision that they want to go to heaven and want Jesus Christ to be their Savior.

THE END OF THE BIBLICALLY STRATEGIZED
SALVATION GOSPEL PRESENTATION WHEN
THE UNSAVED RECEIVE CHRIST

The conclusion of the biblically strategized salvation gospel presentation begins by presenting Romans 10:9 "that if you confess with your mouth the Lord Jesus and believe in your heart that God has raised Him from the dead, you will be saved." This verse quickly leads to the easy conclusion. You have done your job. The unsaved person at this point is ready to accept Jesus as Savior. In just three to four minutes you prepared them for this moment. Now is the time to bring this strategized salvation gospel presentation to its conclusion and lead the unsaved person to immediately pray to accept Jesus as Savior.

THE NEWS AT THE END IS BEING SAVED
MEANS SAVED FROM GOING TO HELL

When you present Romans 10:9, the only interpretation is on what it actually means to be saved. You tell them "Joe, when the bible talks about being saved, it means you must be saved from something, you are saved from going to hell and saved from living this life separated from God." You then immediately say "Let me ask you this, Joe. Would you like to know that you can have eternal life in heaven someday?" They will say "Yes." They all say "yes", sometimes an unsaved person will literally shout out a "Yes!" They have been prepared to want to choose Jesus and heaven, have internally chosen Jesus and heaven and are ready to pray to accept Jesus Christ as their Savior. They are excited, but don't you get excited, stay cool, calm and collected.

DO NOT PAUSE HESITATE OR SLOW DOWN OR ASK QUESTIONS KEEP GOING

The instant that the unsaved person says "Yes" do not hesitate or pause and most certainly do not ask the unsaved person any questions, such as "Do you understand what I mean or what I am saying or "do you really know what you are doing?" You, a witnessing Christian are leading this salvation gospel presentation and are the one in control, so stay in control. Do not open the door for "off the wall" statements or questions that can confuse or change the direction away from leading or winning them to Christ. Simply go to the next step and gently say the following;

You say: "Okay Joe, I'd like to lead you in a short prayer for you to accept Jesus Christ as your Savior, then repent and ask forgiveness for your sins. When you pray, your sins are all forgiven and you will have eternal life in heaven. I will lead the prayer, you just repeat the prayer. Will you pray with me?"

Again, they will all say "Yes," and immediately with no hesitation,

You Say: "Joe, this is your prayer. I will lead the prayer; you repeat the prayer: 'Heavenly Father, I accept Jesus Christ as my Savior. I repent of my sins, I ask you to forgive me of my sins, give me eternal life in heaven and I will seek your will for my life. In Jesus name I pray, Amen.

After an unsaved person has prayed to receive Jesus Christ

as their Savior it is important to give them an affirmation of what they have just done. A good affirming statement is "May God bless you and never forget this date. On this date you confessed Jesus as your Savior by praying to receive Him as your Savior, which is the answer to the question about "when you die and it's time for you to go to heaven." To repent of sin is to go in a new forgiven life in Jesus Christ by having faith in Him and to seek His will for your life, because He has a plan and purpose for you. Your sins are now forgiven and you will have eternal life in heaven. In the future if and when you sin, repent of your sin, ask Him to forgive you and He will. He does not give license to sin. He is the only way to live forgiven and free from the grip of sin. The bible teaches the next step is to find a bible believing church to learn more about Him and grow more deeply in Him. I suggest……(refer them to a church, cell or home group) The second part of the Great Commission is that they should be taught about the things of God, therefore help them to get to your own church or to another bible believing Church.

(The subject of Jesus being raised from the dead as introduced in Romans 10:9 is not presented or discussed except as it is referred to when explaining Romans 6:23. Because it is not dealt with here, do not take that to mean that I do not believe in His bodily resurrection. I absolutely do, because if there is no bodily resurrection, there is no Savior. At this point in the gospel presentation it is not necessary to offer an in-depth explanation of the resurrection to lead or win an unsaved person to Christ.)

YOU CONNECTED ALL THE SALVATION GOSPEL DOTS

All unsaved people know the words "repent and sin." They know a little about Adam and Eve. They are very familiar with the virgin birth, death, burial and resurrection of Jesus Christ. Unsaved people have a general knowledge about these words, names and events, but with the biblically strategized salvation gospel presentation you put everything together for them. You "connected all the salvation dots for them" in a way that they will completely understand, which includes the biblical answer to the "difficult death and danger question." With the biblically strategized salvation gospel presentation unsaved people are prepared to hear and they will hear, the most understandable salvation gospel presentation that they have ever heard. The structure and strategy in this salvation gospel presentation prepares them to instantly want to hear the salvation gospel, As you present this unique gospel presentation, they will hear the salvation gospel presented in a way that they have never heard before. They will relate to it, understand it and will immediately accept Jesus Christ as their Savior.

TWELVE RANDOM TRANSITION STATEMENT EXAMPLES ONLY FOR STUDY

These are some random responses that are only examples of what could be said to an unsaved person when they respond to being asked "Let me ask you this. When you die and it's time for you to go to heaven and Jesus Christ asks you 'Why should I give you eternal life in heaven?' What would you say to Jesus?"

These are a group of responses to help give you a "sense and a feel" of how to respond to whatever the response of an unsaved person may be. Keep in mind, these types of responses are what an unsaved person might state back to a witnessing Christian. These are not to memorize, but are general examples to help you have a feel for how to respond to whatever answers unsaved people may say in response to the death and danger question.

1. I'm a religious person. "That's a normal response. I can tell you are a religious person. Let me share something with you, that the bible says about that for you, today."
2. I believe there are many paths to God. "That's a normal response, because a lot of people believe that there are

many paths to God. Let me share something with you that the bible says about that for you, today."

3. Because I deserve it. "That's a normal response. I think most people like you would like to think they have lived a good life and deserve to go to heaven. Let me share something with you that the bible says about that for you today.

4. I have lived a good life. "That's a normal response from someone who has tried to live a good life. Let me share something with you that the bible says about that for you today."

5. I've never tried to hurt anyone. "That's a normal response for someone like you who is a nice person. Let me share something with you that the bible says about that for you today."

6. I believe everyone goes to heaven. "That's a normal response. A lot of people believe everyone gets to go to heaven. Let me share something with you that the bible says about that for you today."

7. I believe we die and that's it. "That's a normal response, because a lot of people believe that when we die, that's it. Let me share something with you that the bible says about that for you today."

8. I don't care if I go to heaven or not. "That's a normal response. I've talked with other people that felt that way. Let me share something with you that the bible says about that for you today."

9. We are all God's children and he won't send anyone away. "That's a normal response. A lot of people feel the same way. Let me share something with you that the bible says about that for you today."

10. I believe in reincarnation so I don't worry about dying. "That's a normal response. A lot of people believe in reincarnation. Let me share something with you that the bible says about that for you today."

11. I don't believe in God, so It doesn't matter. "That's normal response. Many people say that they don't believe in God. Let me share something with you that the bible says about that for you today."

12. I don't believe in Heaven or Hell. "That's a normal response. Many people say that they don't believe in heaven or hell. Let me share something with you that the bible says about that for you today."

TRANSITION EXAMPLES FROM RANDOM RESPONSES

These are twelve examples of how the transitional statement will work no matter what an unsaved person may say when asked the "death and danger" question. This is why this is a flexible strategized salvation gospel presentation and not a canned gospel presentation.

WILL JESUS ASK WHY SHOULD I GIVE
YOU ETERNAL LIFE IN HEAVEN

Jesus very well could ask "why should I give you eternal life in heaven?" or a variation of this same penetrating question. In Rev 20:11-15 "Then I saw a great white throne and Him who sat on it, from whose face the earth and the heaven fled away. And these found no place for them. And I saw the dead, small and great, standing before God, and books were opened, which is the Book of Life. And the dead were judged according to their works, by the things which were written in the books. The sea gave up the dead who were in it, and Death and Hades delivered up the dead who were in them. And they were judged, each one according to his works. Then Death and Hades were cast into the lake of fire.

This is the second death. And anyone not found in the Book of Life was cast into the lake of fire." The Book of Life contains those who are in Christ. Those who are not will appear at judgement and will perhaps plead in many ways to be let into heaven. Jesus could very well ask something like "why should I give you eternal life in heaven if your name is not written in the Book of Life." This question, as it is presented to unsaved people is powerful, un-nerving and immediately brings them to an extreme awareness of their potential eternal danger. It is a strategic question designed to bring unsaved people to a position of awareness and vulnerability to their eternal danger.

CHAPTER EIGHT

TO LEAD OR WIN AN UNSAVED PERSON
TO CHRIST IS NOT GUESS WORK

Leading unsaved people to Christ consistently is an intentional and prepared Spirit led process. It is not guess work or a chance happening. You may be someone who has led an unsaved person to Christ, but are not sure exactly how it happened and do not know how to do it again. This training will teach you how to lead unsaved people to immediate decisions for Christ for the rest of your life. When witnessing Christians learn to present this salvation gospel presentation all of the traditional evangelism concepts of "deep relationship, personality connection and searching for hidden needs to "minister about" will all fall into peripheral or secondary supportive evangelism concepts. The ultimate solution and foundation for personal evangelism is from one thing. It is for Christians to learn and know "what to say and why to say it, who to say it to, when to say it, where to say it and how to say it" in order to know how to lead or win any unsaved person to Christ.

A FEW ARE KNOWN TO BE ABLE TO LEAD
UNSAVED PEOPLE TO CHRIST

In many churches, there may be a few that are known as men or women that have an ability to lead unsaved people to their decisions for Christ. Some assume that they have a "gift" of evangelism, but this is not true. The bible never states that there is any gifting requirement in order to lead unsaved people to Christ. Over the years, I have spoken with many of these wonderful men and women who can lead unsaved people to immediate decisions for Christ. These fine men and women all have one thing in common. I would ask them, "What do you say or do to lead people to their decision for Christ?" Their answers were almost always identical. They would reply "I don't know, I just do it."

HONEST BUT NOT ACCURATE

I knew that their answers were honest, but not necessarily accurate. I would continue asking more questions or "pick their brain" until I got to the full story. The background was that all of these men and women had been exposed to some form of evangelism teaching or training. They had personally incorporated "evangelism ideas and concepts" from different sources. They then developed some form of a evangelism technique for themselves and from doing that, they led unsaved people to Christ. So, whenever I asked them "the how do you do it question", they would say "I don't know, I just do it". They would answer that way for a specific reason. It was because they could not articulate or explain what they actually said or did to lead an unsaved person to Christ that was consistent or duplicatable. What they said to unsaved people was always similar, sort of on the fly, but not quite the same. This is why they would say "I don't know how I do it, I just do it."

NEVER AGAIN STRESS THINKING "DO I HAVE TO MAKE SOMETHING UP"

The biblically strategized salvation gospel presentation is not a vague, general or "wing it on the fly" gospel presentation. It is intentionally designed to lead unsaved people to immediate decisions for Christ. This gospel presentation will completely eliminate any "I'll have to wing it or make something up" stressful thinking. In all general conversations a witnessing Christian will always have the ability to adjust and shift the conversation into introducing this salvation gospel presentation.

NOW BE PREPARED TO HELP FULFILL THE GREAT COMMISSION

The term or phrase, "The Great Commission", refers to the command and direction in Matt 28: 19-20 and Mark 16: 15-16, that Jesus gave to the body of Christ to make disciples. This is a call and command that cannot be fulfilled without personal evangelism

Matt 28: 18-20 "And Jesus came and spoke to them, saying "All authority has been given to Me in heaven and on earth. Go therefore and make disciples of all the nations, baptizing them in the name of the Father and of the Son and of the Holy Spirt. Teaching them to observe all things that I have commanded you: and lo, I am with you always, even to the end of the age."

Mk 16: 15-16 "Go into all the world and preach the gospel to every creature. He who believes and is baptized will be saved: but he who does not believe will be condemned."

John 3:16 "For God so loved the world that He gave His only begotten Son, that whoever believes in Him should not perish but have everlasting life."

The Great Commission is a global command from Jesus Christ for the body of Christ to go and make disciples by winning every unsaved person on the planet to Christ. God's heart and vision of the Great Commission is to forgive sins, cleanse of sin and make disciples of all saved people to then do His will on a global scale. In John 3:16 Jesus Himself, is telling the body of Christ that God's love and heart for the salvation of His creation is also global. Keep in mind that when Adam and Eve were created, they were sinless and there was no sin in the world. Their act of disobedience brought sin into the world and separated mankind from God spiritually for all eternity. Humanity was separated from God as a result of original sin. This is what brought wickedness and because of their wickedness, God brought the flood. Except for Noah and his family, all people separated from God in sin, died in the flood.

ANSWERS TO HARD QUESTIONS

Many unsaved people say "I cannot believe in God, because a loving God would never send people to hell." Sin, not God takes unsaved people to hell. Unsaved people go to hell because they are separated from God as a result of "original sin" in the Garden of Eden. God cannot and will not be in the presence of sin. Gen 3:22-23 "Then the Lord God said, "Behold, the man has become like one of Us, to know good and evil. And now, lest he put out his hand and take also of the tree of life, and eat, and live forever-therefore the Lord God sent him out of the garden of Eden to till the ground from which he was taken." Some unsaved people refer to the flood in Gen 7:1-24 when God destroyed all living things on the earth. He sent the flood because of their wickedness and that every intent of their hearts was evil as a result of original sin. This is why He sent His Son in order for all unsaved people to receive Christ, have forgiveness of sins and be born again. They also refer to Jos 6:21, when Jericho was destroyed by the Nation of Israel. "And they utterly destroyed all that was in the city, both man and woman, young and old, ox and sheep and donkey, with the edge of the sword." Christians many times have a hard time understanding or giving an answer for these brutal events, but they can be answered and understood. The answer is after the flood the Lord God began anew with His creation through Noah and his family. This led to the coming of Abram, who became Abraham and through him Isaac, then Jacob. God changed Jacob's name to Israel and through him came the Nation of Israel. Later, Moses led and delivered the Nation of Israel out of bondage, brought the law and with it, animal sacrifice and the shedding of animal blood for the sins of the Nation of Israel. After the death of Moses, Joshua became their leader. God had the Nation of Israel led by Joshua, completely destroy cultures of false gods and people of sin to cleanse the land of sin in order to create sinless lands for the Nation of Israel to occupy. All of these events were to make the way for the coming of Jesus Christ and His glorious work on the cross for the sin of all who accept and receive Him as their Savior.

GOD WILL NOT ALLOW PEOPLE OF SIN IN HIS PRESENCE

In the time of Joshua, nations, including its people with their cultures of false gods, were cleansed of sin by the sword. Today, through Jesus Christ and His Great Commission, God is calling for nations globally to be cleansed of sin and unsaved people by winning them to Jesus Christ to be His disciples. What the Nation of Israel did with the sword to eliminate sin in nations, was the forerunner of what fulfilling the Great Commission through evangelism will do today to make disciples of the nations in the name of Jesus Christ. This is why He sent His only begotten Son, Jesus Christ to have the sins forgiven globally, for all who accept and receive Him as their Savior.

WHY ARE THE UNSAVED ACHIEVERS

Some unsaved people will bring up why would God allow Adolph Hitler, Joseph Stalin or Mao Zedong to kill so many people? He gave His creation free will, the ability to make decisions, both good or bad. God did not make robots. The answer is they were all part of humanity that was created in the image of God. This gives authority to both the saved and unsaved to be people that have human authority, as a result of being created in God's image to become achievers. Unfortunately, these were men who achieved evil things. They accomplished not in the name of God, but by being demonically led, with their own anti-Christ goals. This reference about these evil men, is also to help explain why "it doesn't seem fair" that so many unsaved people achieve, gain success and many Christians do not gain a high level of success. This brief overview is to help prepare you with an answer whenever unsaved people question, judge or attack God or the people of God on this subject.

Matt 5:45b "for He makes His sun rise on the evil and on the good, and sends rain on the just and on the unjust."

Fulfilling the Great Commission is God's calling for the entire body of Christ, which absolutely includes you. When you learn the biblically strategized salvation gospel presentation you will be fully equipped and prepared to do your part to fulfill the Great Commission. The place to start is with your unsaved family members, friends or an occasional stranger. Learn, pray to be led and the Holy Spirit or an Angel will lead you to the people, young or old, to win to Christ.

THE ANSWER TO EVERY RELIGIOUS, CULTURAL, SOCIAL AND GENDER CHALLENGE

A large part of what the Great Commission fulfills is that in Christ all are equal and humanity should view itself as equal. This worldview is clarified in Gal 3:26-28 and is the answer to all of the fundamental problems that humanity struggles with on a daily basis. Jesus Christ is the way to heal and resolve every religious, cultural, racial, social and gender challenge throughout the world. The world wants answers to these problems and the only answer is salvation in Jesus Christ.

"For you are all sons of God through faith in Christ Jesus. For as many of you as were baptized into Christ have put on Christ. There is neither Jew, nor Greek, there is neither slave nor free, there is neither male nor female; for you are all one in Christ Jesus."

TO PREACH MEANS PRESENT CHRIST WITH A STRATEGY TO WIN TO CHRIST

To go into all the world and make disciples means leading unsaved people to Christ. To then teach them is what discipleship is to accomplish. The word "preach" is simply a word that specifies a targeted evangelism intent. Evangelistically, the word "preach" means to be prepared to introduce, present and conclude the salvation gospel of Jesus Christ with an immediate salvation result. It also means that having a planned salvation gospel presentation will eliminate confusion, so any Christian will know "what to say and why to say it, who to say it to, when to say it, where to say it and how to say it" in order to know how to introduce, present and conclude the salvation gospel with immediate salvation results. To preach does not mean to have general heartfelt witnessing conversations with no salvation results.

Rom 10:14 "How then shall they call on Him in whom they have not heard? And how shall they hear without a preacher?" This is a clarion call for the entire body of Christ as any Christian can preach a salvation gospel message in personal evangelism. This clarion call, mirrors the call in the Great Commission to "go and make disciples." The body of Christ cannot fulfill the Great Commission, which is a call, primarily for personal evangelism, unless men, women and mature teens know how to win souls. The biblically strategized salvation gospel presentation will fill that need. With it, men, women and mature teens will be prepared and equipped to lead millions of unsaved people to immediate decisions for Christ. It is the structure, strategy and goal in this unique personal evangelism salvation gospel presentation that makes it a form of what is considered preaching.

General witnessing is quite good, fine, and normal when appropriate. However, men, women and mature teens need to have the ability to balance general witnessing with the ability, as the Lord leads, to shift and transfer into presenting the biblically strategized salvation gospel presentation. This means to memorize, learn and know the biblically strategized salvation gospel presentation in order to know precisely how to introduce, present and conclude the salvation gospel with immediate salvation results. Don't let the word preach concern you. It is simply a word that means to strategically present the salvation gospel of Jesus' Christ with a designed conclusion to lead an unsaved person to immediately accept Jesus Christ as their Savior. This is exactly what the biblically strategized salvation gospel presentation is designed to give men, women and mature teens the ability to do in personal evangelism.

PREACHING OR PRESENTING CHRIST CAN TAKE PLACE ANYWHERE AND ANYTIME

Christians generally assume or think of "preaching" as something done by a speaker from a pulpit or a platform, but that is a misconception. In personal or individual evangelism presenting the salvation gospel to an unsaved person is not from a pulpit, but is done person to person in any number of places. Presenting Christ in personal evangelism can take place riding in a car, standing in a parking lot, sitting at a table in a coffee shop, in the lunch room or the board room, on the telephone or in endless locations. This is what the biblically strategized salvation gospel presentation enables you to consistently do in personal evangelism. One of the most "positive, comforting and reassuring" features of this unique gospel presentation is that it does not sound "preachy." It is low-key, non-threating, non-condemning, very interesting, understandable and all unsaved people want to hear it.

THE APOSTLE PAUL TELLS THE BODY OF
CHRIST TO PERSUADE THE UNSAVED

In personal evangelism to persuade is convincing an unsaved person to accept and receive Jesus Christ as their own Savior. This is what the Great Commission means when it tells the body of Christ to make disciples. Every Christian is going to be rewarded for what they do.

2Cor5:10-11 "For we must all appear before the judgment seat of Christ, that each one may receive the things done in the body, according to what he has done, whether good or bad. Knowing therefore, the terror of the Lord, we persuade men, but we are well known to God, and I also trust are well known in your consciences."

BE PREPARED TO INSTANTLY PRESENT THE BIBLICALLY
STRATEGIZED SALVATION GOSPEL PRESENTATION

One of the things that the Apostle Paul underscored is to always be prepared to win an unsaved person to Christ. The Lord can lead you to lead an unsaved person to Christ in less than ideal circumstances and you need to be prepared. I once led an extremely wealthy 88 year old woman to Christ in the middle of a wedding reception. The Lord led me and I led her. It is that simple. You and I need to be prepared at all times to lead an unsaved person to Christ. With the biblically strategized salvation gospel presentation you will be prepared to immediately lead unsaved people to Christ in any situation.

IF YOU ARE MARRIED TO AN UNSAVED PERSON

To be married to an unsaved person is a sensitive and challenging situation for any Christian man or woman. If there has been contention over the things of God, then back off. If there has been "nagging" to go to church or to accept Jesus, back off. If you can, apologize for any aggressive "witnessing, put downs or nagging." Pray for them, let the Lord and some time bring a level of healing and calm. Learn the biblically strategized salvation gospel presentation. Be prepared to wait on the Lord for the right moment to present this salvation gospel presentation. When you do, you will then be able to calmly, lovingly and gently, lead them to accept Jesus Christ as their Savior.

DO NOT FANTASIZE ABOUT UNREALISTIC EVANGELISM CIRCUMSTANCES

2Tim 4:1-5 "Preach the word! Be ready in season and out of season. Convince, rebuke, exhort, with all longsuffering and teaching. For the time will come when they will not endure sound doctrine, but according to their own desires, because they have itching ears, they will heap up for themselves teachers; and they will turn their ears away from the truth and be turned aside to fables. But you be watchful in all things, endure afflictions, do the work of an evangelist, fulfill your ministry."

This penetrating scripture tells us that not all evangelistic opportunities, conditions or circumstances are going to be ideal and Christians need to be prepared for non-ideal conditions and circumstances when they arise. This is critical, because as the bible teaches, many unsaved people will believe almost anything. (these are the fables) This is why it is so important to understandably present the word of God. The difference in "preach the word and go witness or share your faith" is simple.

To preach in personal evangelism is to present the salvation gospel, being led of the Holy Spirt or an Angel in a planned and organized manner. To witness or share your faith has no direction goal or strategy and no planned conclusion. It is similar to "throwing mud against the wall to see what sticks." The power of the biblically strategized salvation gospel presentation is that it is organized with a planned salvation conclusion. After they learn this one of a kind salvation gospel presentation, men, women and mature teens will always be ready and prepared to lead unsaved people to Christ, no matter what the conditions or circumstances happen to be.

The Apostle Paul emphatically proclaimed "Preach the word! Be ready in season and out of season" for a very specific reason. Preaching about any subject is always from a prepared, structured and strategized message. It always has an introduction, presentation and conclusion, irrespective if it is from a platform or in person. In personal evangelism, preach the word to be ready in season and out of season, means to already know what to present that is planned, structured and strategized. This is in order to be prepared to present the salvation gospel of Jesus Christ to unsaved people, no matter what the circumstances happen to be. This is the only way to always be prepared and know precisely what to say in order to consistently introduce, present and conclude presenting the salvation gospel with an immediate salvation result. This is what learning the biblically strategized salvation gospel presentation will do for you.

CHAPTER NINE

CHRISTIANS ARE TO WARN AND WIN TO CHRIST

The primary goal for witnessing Christians in doing the work of an evangelist is to lead or win unsaved people to their decision for Christ. In the process of leading or winning unsaved people to Christ with this salvation gospel presentation, unsaved people are gently warned of the danger they are in of going to hell. Whenever a witnessing Christian presents this salvation gospel presentation, they warn unsaved people about the danger of hell in the most sensitive way possible.

Col 1:28 "Him we preach, warning every man and teaching every man in all wisdom, that we may present every man perfect in Christ Jesus."

TO WIN AN UNSAVED PERSON TO CHRIST BRINGS RECONCILIATION

Reconciliation is what the Lord God wants for His creation. The fundamental problem that all of humanity has is being spiritually separated from God as a result of original sin. When a man, woman or mature teen lead's an unsaved person to Christ they are being used of God in the glorious work of winning unsaved people into being reconciled back to God.

2 Corinthians 5:18-20 "Now all things are of God, who has reconciled us to Himself through Jesus Christ, and has given us the ministry of reconciliation, that is, that God was in Christ reconciling the world to Himself, not imputing their trespasses to them, and has committed to us the word of reconciliation. Now then, we are ambassadors for Christ, as though God were pleading through us; we implore you on Christ's behalf, be reconciled to God."

The mission of an ambassador is to sensitively and diplomatically convey the message they are charged to deliver. Every Christian is an ambassador for Christ. You will discover that the biblically strategized salvation gospel presentation is an incredibly sensitive and diplomatic way to introduce, present and conclude the salvation gospel of Jesus Christ with an immediate salvation result.

PRAY FOR THE LORD TO PREPARE
UNSAVED FAMILY AND FRIENDS

Pray for unsaved family members and friends. Ask the Lord to prepare your unsaved family members and friends to be available to hear and receive the salvation gospel of Jesus Christ. If you do, the Lord will go before you and minister to them to be available and prepared to receive this salvation gospel presentation and Jesus as their Savior. Trust Him and He will always be there for both you and your unsaved family members or friends. The role of a Christian is not to try and be the Holy Spirit in the life of any unsaved person by condemning them or their behavior, thinking they can "convict them" of wrong doing.

James 5:16C "The effective fervent prayer of a righteous man avails much."

MANY HAVE BEEN WINNING THE UNSAVED
TO DECISIONS JUST NOT TO CHRIST

In personal evangelism over the years, millions of Christians have been winning or attempting to win unsaved people to decisions, just not to decisions to receive Jesus as their Savior. They have been winning unsaved people to make decisions to visit their church, a home group or attend a crusade. They win them to different kinds of Christian "events, functions or services" to hopefully be won to Christ by a "perceived more qualified person." In the mind of most Christians a "more qualified person" is probably the Sr. pastor or any staff pastor, but this could also include a Sunday School teacher, a home group or cell leader. When men, women and mature teens learn this one of a kind structured and strategized salvation gospel presentation they will never again think they have to win or invite an unsaved person to a Christian gathering to be led to Christ by a "perceived more qualified person."

TO LIVE A FULFILLED LIFE IS A LIFE
THAT INCLUDES WINNING SOULS

This text is in a letter that may have been addressed to Timothy, but it was written for the entire body of Christ. It is for Christians to make a commitment to do the work of an evangelist. Some Christians may feel unfulfilled, as if something is missing or lacking in their lives. The deep thing that is missing is doing the work of an evangelist by leading unsaved people to Christ in personal evangelism. This is because the lifelong personal ministry calling of every Christian is to fulfill the Great Commission by doing the work of an evangelist. They attend church, are told to "witness" or hear testimonies about how others witnessed. To go beyond being only a hearer and become a doer is to start leading unsaved people to Christ. The Apostle Paul states that this is the way to have a fulfilled life in serving the Lord. Doing the work of an evangelist takes Christians out of the "bleachers as a hearer and on to the playing field as a doer." The playing field is your personal evangelism mission field, which includes unsaved family members, friends or occasional strangers. With the biblically strategized salvation gospel presentation you will completely be prepared to be a doer, out of the bleachers and no longer just an hearer or observer in the body of Christ. You will quickly discover a fulfillment in your Christian life that you never dreamed possible for yourself. This does not mean you are called to be an evangelist, but are called to do the work of an evangelist. James 1:22 "But be doers of the word, and not hearers only, deceiving yourselves."

2Timothy 4:5 "But you be watchful in all things, endure afflictions, do the work of an evangelist, fulfill your ministry.

YOU WILL NOT KNOW WHAT YOU ARE DOING
UNTIL YOU KNOW WHAT TO SAY

When you learn the biblically strategized salvation gospel presentation, you will know at all times and circumstances what to say and do in personal evangelism. Traditional witnessing ideas will immediately become supportive type generalized statements that should be non-controversial and limited conversation about the things of God. The personal evangelism goal for every Christian should be to actually lead unsaved people to their immediate decisions for Christ. Unless men, women and mature teens are prepared with this salvation gospel presentation their attempts at personal evangelism are largely based on "uncertain guess work" and this is why most Christians do not evangelize.

UNSAVED PEOPLE DO NOT LIKE TO BE
TOLD BUT ARE WILLING TO BE LED

In personal evangelism, unsaved people do not want to be told what to do, but they are all willing to be led into what to do. This is the fundament difference between over aggressive general witnessing with no goal, structure or direction and gently presenting Jesus Christ with the biblically strategized salvation gospel presentation. Many times, traditional witnessing with no goal, direction or strategy can quickly get out of control and ends up with some Christians trying to "argue, push, drive or even intimidate" unsaved people to decisions for Christ. A lot of general witnessing with no structure is a "fire, ready, aim" process with no decisions for Christ. At times, some witnessing can sound "like a Christian is talking down to unsaved people, condemning, criticizing or lecturing them."

SOME TRY TO TELL ABOUT JESUS WHEN THE UNSAVED DON'T WANT TO HEAR IT

Too often, well intentioned Christians try to tell unsaved people things about Jesus Christ and salvation, before an unsaved person is ready to hear or receive what a Christian wants to tell them. The whole idea of creating a teachable moment by preparing unsaved people to instantly want hear the salvation gospel of Jesus Christ is for a specific reason. It is to present the salvation gospel to them when they have been prepared to want hear it and are then willing to hear it.

MANY LIVE IN QUIET DESPERATION BECAUSE THEY DON'T KNOW WHAT TO SAY OR DO

Many Christian men and women live lives of quiet evangelism desperation. They know that faith, trust and belief in Jesus Christ is the only way to salvation and eternal life in heaven. Their frustration and desperation is knowing that they cannot present or explain the salvation gospel of Jesus Christ to unsaved family members or friends in a way that would lead any of them to immediately receive Jesus as Savior. If you have unsaved family members or friends over the age of twenty-two the odds of them receiving Jesus as Savior become more doubtful and remote. Most Christians accept Jesus as Savior before the age of twenty-one. It is horrific to imagine a beloved family member or friend going to hell. They may be wonderful people, but if they have not received Jesus as Savior, when they die, they will be lost forever. If you have unsaved family members or friends in their mid-twenties and older, be encouraged. You will be able to lead them to their salvation in Jesus Christ with this biblically strategized salvation gospel presentation.

ALL CHRISTIANS KNOW THE BASIC SALVATION STORY

All Christians know and understand what Jesus did on the cross. What many do not know is how to present what Jesus did on the cross in an organized and understandable way that leads an unsaved person to want to receive Him as Savior. Well intentioned men or women and mature teens that tell an unsaved person about Jesus and get no salvation commitment or response can then become very frustrated, very fast.

This is primarily from participating in "vague or general witnessing situations" prepared with only an "I'm right, You're wrong" attitude. All Christians know Jn 14:6 "I am the way the truth and the life. No one comes to the Father except through Me." It is one thing for Christians to righteously believe and know that the only way to salvation is to accept and receive Jesus Christ as Savior. It is another thing to witness or interact with any unsaved person armed and prepared with only an "I'm right, You're wrong" attitude.

It is this kind of attitude that creates an aggressive willingness to insensitively confront, argue or attempt to intimidate unsaved people into receiving or agreeing with whatever is being presented to them. The biblically strategized salvation gospel presentation will eliminate and solve all of these unnecessary and predictably, argumentative confrontations. If you have been in witnessing experiences that ended up in arguments or fights and never want them to happen again, then this salvation gospel presentation is for you.

WHAT TO DO WHEN PEOPLE SAY THAT THEY DO NOT BELIEVE IN THE BIBLE GOD JESUS HEAVEN OR HELL

Most Christians are caught "off guard" and are very uncomfortable about what to say and do, whenever they hear someone say "I don't believe in God, Jesus Christ, Heaven, Hell or the Bible." A statement like this could come in a general conversation with several people present or in a one on one conversation when a Christian is trying to witness. In a public setting, in the midst of a general conversation about "religious things" just ignore it. Don't let yourself get drawn into a "public witnessing argument brawl." The biblically strategized salvation gospel presentation that you will learn, has a strategy built into it that anticipates these kinds of comments from unsaved people. When you learn this strategized salvation gospel presentation, then if a situation like this arises, stay cool, calm and collected and pray for a private opportunity to talk with the particular person making the statement and the others that overheard these anti-God, anti-Christ comments. Unsaved people that make these kinds of comments usually don't have a deep commitment to being an atheist. Generally speaking, they do not know what they believe, so they make these kinds of statements to validate a sort of "with it" persona. Actually, unsaved people that make these kinds of statements, have no depth of belief in what they say and are very easy to lead to a decision for Christ.

DO NOT FOCUS ON SELF OR GENERAL PROBLEMS

When Christians want to witness and focus on "hot button or felt need" issues, witnessing can start and get out of control quite quickly. This is because most potential answers to general life problems are matters of opinion, which can be contentious and lead to arguments. Most life problems or issues deal with family, work, different relationships, perhaps different types of addiction, but the list can go on and on. Most Christians want to be relational and want unsaved people to know that they understand and have a concern. A Christian may have experienced a similar problem and want them to know that their faith in Jesus Christ got them through and if the unsaved person accepts Jesus as their Savior, He will get them through as well. The subliminal message can make an unsaved person think "If I accept Jesus, will I become like you?" No disrespect to anyone, but "They may like you, but they do not want to be you."

UNSAVED PEOPLE CAN SAY ANYTHING AND SLIP AWAY

This contributes to why some unsaved people may take the position of "You are you and I am I, so you live your life and I'll live mine." An unsaved person could say "Your religious life is good for you, but not for me." Generalized witnessing with no specific direction, goal, structure, strategy or designed conclusion can easily end with unsaved people "walking away" with no decision for Christ. Unsaved people can say many things in order to "get away or slip away" from a general witnessing Christian. A witnessing Christian then wonders "why didn't they believe me and do what I wanted them to do or what did I say wrong or what else should I have said." Some Christians after one of these type encounters leave thinking "I told them what they need know, I shared the Lord with them and I feel I gave a deep and powerful witness." Some may think "I did my Christian duty" If an unsaved person walks away from a general witness encounter and is killed in a car wreck or has a stroke or heart attack and dies, what good is a deep and powerful general witness conversation? The biblically strategized salvation gospel presentation completely prevents these kinds of problems from coming up and will solve the full range of these witnessing type problems.

NO MATTER WHAT THE PROBLEM INTRODUCE THE BIBLICALLY STRATEGIZED SALVATION GOSPEL PRESENTATION

Witnessing to discover "hot button or felt need" problems to present Jesus Christ as Savior has been passed down from one ministry generation to the next for decades. This is why in the 21st Century, most Christians have no idea how to win or lead any unsaved person to a decision to accept and receive Jesus as their Savior. When Christians learn the biblically strategized salvation gospel presentation with its initial focus on death and eternal life issues, they will see arguments disappear. It does not matter what an unsaved person's outward life issues happen to be, because Jesus Christ did not go to the cross to solve personal problems. He went to the cross to take upon Himself the sin of the world and save all those who accept and receive Him as their Savior. It does not matter what an unsaved person thinks, has opinions of or thinks they believe. This is because no matter what they think they know or believe, whatever it is, it will change once you present this one of a kind salvation gospel presentation. This is why no matter what any Christian may think is or seems to be a priority problem for any unsaved person, their new priority will become their own salvation in Jesus Christ and eternal life in Heaven.

UNSAVED PEOPLE HAVE NO SPIRITUAL PRIORITIES UNTIL YOU EXPLAIN THAT YES THEY DO

Do not think that an unsaved person has a priority on what problems they want solved first. When you learn to introduce and present this unique salvation gospel presentation, unsaved people immediately realize that their true first priority is to receive Jesus as their Savior, have their sins forgiven and have eternal life in heaven. This is why it is so important to transform personal evangelism thinking from vague generalized "hot button, felt need" issues to focus on the most important issues of life, which are Jesus Christ, salvation and eternal life.

GIVE UNSAVED PEOPLE AN OPPORTUNITY
TO MAKE THEIR DECISION FOR CHRIST

When men, women and mature teens learn the biblically strategized salvation gospel presentation, they will be prepared to introduce, present and conclude the salvation gospel with an immediate salvation result. This is the biblical way to consistently give unsaved people an opportunity to make their decision for Christ. This salvation gospel presentation explains the salvation gospel of Jesus Christ in a way that unsaved people "understand it and identify with it". Upon hearing this unique salvation gospel presentation, 95% to 100% of the unsaved people that hear it from you will immediately pray to receive Jesus Christ as their Savior.

That is the exact opposite of unsaved people "possibly" being asked to make their decision for Christ, but from only hearing "general, unrelatable, vague or directionless witnessing." Being unprepared to introduce, present and conclude the salvation gospel with an immediate salvation result is why approximately 95% of all Christians have never led or won a single unsaved person to Christ.

CHAPTER TEN

A TEACHING TO EQUIP AND PREPARE EVERYONE

Several years ago, a young woman, that did domestic work, attended one of my seminars on "How to win Souls." She did not have an automobile and rode the bus to her work. She leads people to Christ with the biblically strategized salvation gospel presentation on the bus with ease and then directs them to her church. The only thing that is required to learn how to win souls in personal evangelism is the desire and willingness to learn the salvation gospel presentation to then be prepared to be a participant in fulfilling the Great Commission.

THE TEACHING AND ANALYSIS IS FOR ALL CHRISTIANS

You may be shocked as you become more aware of the primary reason that most personal evangelism is shut down. It is the same problem throughout the entire body of Christ. You will discover and learn that the solution to these various, but similar problems is quite simple and uncomplicated. Over the years I have spoken with countless numbers of Christians about their views, concerns and fears about personal evangelism. In different ways, they all said the same thing. Their main personal evangelistic concern is "I don't know what to say or should say to an unsaved person."

THE PERSONAL EVANGELISM PROBLEM IS SOLVED

I have heard many mature Christians speculate about why most Christians do not witness, care to witness and cannot lead any unsaved people to Christ. Some have stated that they think Christians just don't care about unsaved people. I think a more realistic view is that most Christians just don't know what to say to unsaved people in personal evangelism. So they just avoid evangelism to feel safe and secure.

SATAN ATTACKS WHEN CHRISTIANS DO NOT KNOW WHAT TO SAY OR DO

When Christians do not know what to say and do, Satan attacks with fear. He attacks with the fear of the unknown, the fear of rejection and fear of failure. This is spiritual warfare. Satan attacks with negative thoughts and ideas, but you have authority over him and can command him to instantly stop his attack upon you. You have biblical authority to say: "In the name of Jesus Christ, Satan I command you to stop attacking me with fear of the unknown, failure, rejection, frustration, low self-esteem and now get behind me. In the name of Jesus Christ, I cast you out and command you to get behind me and away from me."

Mk 16:17ab "And these signs will follow those who believe. In my name they will cast out demons;" 1Pet 5:8-9 "Be sober, be vigilant; because your adversary the devil walks about like a roaring lion, seeking whom he may devour. Resist him, steadfast in the faith, knowing that the same sufferings are experienced by your brotherhood in the world."

YOU CAN FIGHT THE LIE OF THE DEVIL

When you learn this one of a kind uniquely structured and strategized salvation gospel presentation, you will have a strong, sound and prepared evangelistic mind to lead unsaved people to Christ. Satan will have no evangelical place to attack you. The powerful and assuring evangelism reality is that once you learn this salvation gospel presentation, you will never again have to be concerned about what to say to an unsaved person.

2Tim1:7 "For "God has not given us a spirit of fear, but of power and of love and of a sound mind."

THIS ONE OF A KIND SALVATION GOSPEL PRESENTATION IS YOUR BIBLICAL ARMOR

Unsaved people are never the enemy. The goal is not to defeat them, but to lead them to Christ. To overcome the attacks of Satan in personal evangelism men, women and mature teens can now be completely secure in their evangelism. This one of a kind biblically strategized salvation gospel presentation is your personal evangelism armor.

Eph 6:10-13 "Finally, my brethren, be strong in the Lord and in the power of His might. Put on the whole armor of God that you may be able to stand against the wiles of the devil. For we do not wrestle against flesh and blood, but against principalities, against powers, against the rulers of the darkness of this age, against spiritual hosts of wickedness in the heavenly places. Therefore, take up the whole armor of God, that you may be able to withstand in the evil day, and having done all to stand."

LEARNING TO LEAD UNSAVED PEOPLE TO CHRIST ELEVATES EVANGELISM THOUGHT

A whole new evangelism world and life in Christ will open for you. This training will lift you above thinking that "effective witnessing" or leading an unsaved person to Christ, is reliant on the perceived depth of a relationship or personality connection. It will eliminate the stress of thinking that the "evangelism goal" is endlessly trying to discover the emotional or hidden current "felt" needs of an unsaved person or some "hot button issue" in order to "figure out" how to "effectively witness" to them. The relationship between a Christian and an unbeliever is a sensitive one and one or the other will be the influencer. This is why Christians must always use caution and wisdom around unsaved people, irrespective of the level of relationship.

OVERWHELMED INTIMIDATED AND CONFUSED BY TRADITIONAL PERSONAL EVANGELISM IDEAS

Most of the body of Christ has never led a single person to Christ. I encourage you to learn how to lead any unsaved person to Christ with the biblically strategized salvation gospel presentation. When you do, your worldview of what to do with unsaved people will immediately and dramatically change. The bible is crystal clear, Christians do not have to make an unsaved person their "new best friend" in order to lead them to their decision for Christ. At times, it can be challenging for Christians to build "deep and meaningful" relationships, even with other Christians. Some leaders teach to build "deep and meaningful" relationships with unsaved people to effectively witness, but with no end in sight.

TRUST PRESENTING THE WORD OF GOD NOT IN NON FELLOWSHIP RELATIONSHIPS

Most Christians are completely overwhelmed, intimidated and confused at the concept of making evangelistic commitments to pursue "deep and meaningful relationships with unsaved people. A deep and meaningful relationship between Christians is "fellowship." This is from being in one accord that Jesus Christ is and He alone is Savior and Lord. Any relationship between a Christian and an unsaved person is in the flesh. A Christian may not be in the flesh, but all unsaved people are in the flesh. The concept or goal of building relationships with unsaved people is primarily from the idea of "making a friend that you could invite to church." On a good, better, best scale, the best thing to do is first lead or win an unsaved person to Christ with the biblically strategized salvation gospel presentation. Men, women and mature teens can then develop a real relationship of fellowship and then invite them to church to be discipled and grow in the Lord. Most Christians are completely overwhelmed, intimidated and confused at the evangelistic concept of making commitments to pursue directionless "deep and meaningful" relationships with unsaved people, without knowing what to say to them evangelistically.

A fundamental problem from an over emphasis on thinking that there must be a deep or meaningful relationship with an unsaved person "as the key to effectively witness" is that it can actually create an unintended relational problem. The problem is that it can create a "fear of witnessing" out of a fear of saying the wrong thing that might offend an unsaved person and jeopardize the relationship. This is a subtle, but significant factor as to why many are hesitant to witness. If an unsaved person tells a Christian they are willing to be friends, but don't discuss "religion" with them, then the wrong person is controlling what can or cannot be discussed about the things of God. The strategized salvation gospel presentation eliminates all of these kinds of problems.

TOLD TO WIN THE WORLD BUT ARE NOT TOLD HOW TO WIN THE WORLD

In evangelism services men, women and mature teens can get enthusiastic and excited about going out to witness to everyone. It does not matter how excited or enthused Christians can get. If they do not know what to say to unsaved people, fear, doubt and confusion are overwhelming challenges for almost all Christians. For many, when they leave the safety of a service and get out into the real world, it feels safe and non-threatening to do nothing.

THE BIBLICALLY STRATEGIZED SALVATION GOSPEL PRESENTATION IS NOT LONG

Men, women and mature teens are comfortable presenting the biblically strategized salvation gospel presentation and unsaved people are always comfortable hearing it, because it is designed to be presented briefly, in a lovingly gentle and low-key manner. Gal 5:22 "But the fruit of the Spirit is love, joy, peace, longsuffering, kindness, goodness, faithfulness, gentleness, self-control. Against such there is no law." Pulpit preaching generally can last thirty minutes to two hours or more, depending on the church or denomination. The biblically strategized salvation gospel presentation that you are about to learn only takes 3-4 minutes.

CHAPTER ELEVEN

WHAT ONE CAN DO IN EVANGELISM
ANOTHER CAN LEARN TO DO

The Apostle Paul wrote most of the New Testament. Paul introduced the spiritual reality that evangelism is about winning unsaved people to Christ and away from Satan in a contest for souls. He wrote metaphorically of winning people to Christ using athletic examples. In the bible, there is only one example of a Christian who led an unsaved person to a decision for Christ and it is not the Apostle Paul. Many believe and teach that Paul led the Philippian Jailer to Christ and this may shock you, but he did not. Let's take a closer look at what actually happened between Paul and the Philippian jailer.

Acts 16:25-31 "But at midnight Paul and Silas were praying and singing hymns to God, and the prisoners were listening to them. Suddenly there was a great earthquake, so that the foundations of the prison were shaken; and immediately all the doors were opened and everyone's chains were loosed. And the keeper of the prison, awaking from sleep and seeing the prison doors open, supposing the prisoners had fled, drew his sword and was about to kill himself. But Paul called with a loud voice, saying, "Do yourself no harm, for we are all here." Then he called for a light, ran in, and fell down trembling before Paul and Silas. And he brought them out and said, "Sirs, what must I do to be saved?" So they said, "Believe on the Lord Jesus Christ, and you will be saved, you and your household."

PAUL STOPPED THE JAILER FROM SUICIDE BUT DID NOT LEAD HIM TO CHRIST

The Apostle Paul stopped the jailer from committing suicide, thereby saving his life, but he did not lead him to Christ. It was Paul and Silas in perfect unison, saying together "So they said. 'Believe on the Lord Jesus Christ, and you will be saved, you and your household." They both told the jailer, as one voice, what he needed to do to get saved. Paul did not "personally" lead or win the unsaved jailer to Christ. It was Paul and Silas together. Paul and Silas in unison, both led him to Christ. This training is for individual personal evangelism and there will be no evangelism partner with you, other than the Holy Spirit or an Angel. It is critically important to learn this unique gospel presentation word for word, because then there will be no insecurity, pause, hesitation or confusion about what to say to any unsaved person.

ONLY PHILIP THE EVANGELIST MODELED HOW TO WIN SOULS

Philip the evangelist, is the biblical personal evangelism role model for the body of Christ. He is the only Christian in the bible that intentionally led an unsaved person to Christ and he did it, strategically. He strategically led the Ethiopian eunuch to salvation in Jesus Christ in a way that is duplicated with the biblically strategized salvation gospel presentation. This one of a kind salvation gospel presentation that you will learn duplicates how the bible demonstrates through Phillip, exactly how to immediately lead unsaved people to decisions for Christ.

LEARN WHAT THE BIBLE TEACHES
ABOUT HOW TO WIN SOULS

As we look closely at this role model text, we can see that Phillip was first of all, led by an Angel, later referred to as a Spirit of the Lord. Philip was led and used of the Lord as a model for the body of Christ, because Philip had a strategized salvation gospel presentation that he could use at a moment's notice. The interaction between Philip and the Ethiopian eunuch models an evangelistic strategy that could be duplicated anywhere in the world in any century of history. The Lord will also let you know through an Angel or the Holy Spirit, when to present the biblically strategized salvation gospel presentation to your unsaved family members, friends and perhaps an occasional stranger. You are also going to learn how to know when the Holy Spirit or an Angel is letting you know, who and when to present the biblically strategized salvation gospel presentation. Philip, the biblical role model for how to lead or win unsaved people to Christ, was led by the Spirit of the Lord, because he was evangelistically prepared. He was prepared to immediately lead or win any unsaved person to Christ and is why the Lord used him to be the personal evangelism role model for the body of Christ.

Acts 8:26-37 "Now an angel of the Lord spoke to Philip, saying, "Arise and go toward the south along the road which goes down from Jerusalem to Gaze." This is desert. So he arose and went. And Behold, a man of Ethiopia, a eunuch of great authority under Candace the queen of the Ethiopians, who had charge of all her treasury, and had come to Jerusalem to worship, was returning. And sitting in his chariot, he was reading Isaiah the Prophet. Then the Spirit said to Philip, "Go near and overtake this chariot." So Philip ran to him, and heard him reading the prophet Isaiah, and said "Do you understand what you are reading?" And he said, "How can I, unless someone guides me." And he asked Philip to come up and sit with him. The place in the Scripture which he read was this:

"He was led as a sheep to the slaughter; And as a lamb before its shearer is silent. So He opened not His mouth. In His humiliation His justice was taken away. And who will declare His generation? For His life is taken from the earth". So the eunuch answered Philip and said, "I ask you, of whom does the prophet say this, of himself or of some other man?" Then Philip opened his mouth, and beginning at this scripture, preached Jesus to him. Now as they went down the road, they came to some water. And the eunuch said, "See here is water. What hinders me from being baptized?" Then Philip said, "If you believe with all your heart, you may." And he answered and said. "I believe that Jesus Christ is the Son of God." So he commanded the chariot to stand still. Both Philip and the eunuch went down into the water and he baptized him. Now when they came up out of the water, the Spirit of the Lord caught Philip away, so that the eunuch saw him no more and he went on his way rejoicing. But Philip was found at Azotus. And passing through, he preached in all the cities till he came to Caesarea."

ALL UNSAVED PEOPLE HAVE CONCERNS ABOUT DEATH

Philip's personal evangelism strategy was simple and uncomplicated. Philip would simply ask unsaved Jews as he introduced Isaiah's prophetic word about Christ and His death, "Do you understand what you are reading? or Do you understand what this means? or Do you understand what Isaiah is telling Jews?" These are speculative type questions, but he absolutely developed a "question style" way to introduce the salvation gospel. His salvation gospel presentation style would have been based upon what Jesus Christ came to do and how His death would impact the death of all of humanity.

Philip had a strategized salvation gospel presentation and the Lord purposely modeled him and his strategic style of leading Jews and in this case, a Gentile to salvation in Jesus Christ. In Acts 8:29 "Now when they came up out of the water, the Spirit of the Lord caught Philip away, so the eunuch saw him no more, and he went on his way rejoicing." We read that the Lord "caught Philip away", which is how the Lord gloriously demonstrated and affirmed that He, the Lord Himself, was leading Philip and was with Philip in the midst of all that he was evangelistically modeling.

PHILIP KNEW WHAT TO SAY STRATEGICALLY

Philip's evangelistic strategy was to first "ask a penetrating evangelistically leading question" in order to prepare any unsaved person, Jew or Gentile, to want to hear the answer, which will be to introduce the salvation gospel. Philip asked and framed his penetrating question a certain way. That certain way is so an unsaved person understands the "deeper implication" in the question, is that the Christian asking the question knows the answer to the penetrating question being asked.

A POWERFUL EVANGELISM ROLE MODEL
FOR THE BODY OF CHRIST

Philip was prepared and had been leading Jews to Christ and because of his experience and "strategic approach to evangelism" was led of the Spirit to the eunuch. The Spirit of the Lord led him to go down a desert road. Philip did not argue, complain or pray about "Is this really you Lord or should I do this or not?" No, Philip did not argue or complain, but was obedient and went down the road. On the road Philip saw the eunuch's chariot and probably other wagons or carts for support staff. The eunuch's chariot would not have been an ordinary chariot. It would have probably been a large and elaborate traveling chariot. This was the chariot of one of the most important men from Ethiopia. He had charge of the Ethiopian treasury. Candace, the Queen of Ethiopia, would have made sure he traveled in great safety and comfort with drivers and staff. This would have been a long six month round trip, tiresome and dangerous journey. In contemporary American political terms, the eunuch was her "Secretary of the Treasury."

PHILIP WAS NOT INTIMIDATED BY WORLDLY PERCEPTIONS

Phillip would have seen the distinctive chariot and all of the security personnel and attendants from a distance when the Spirit told him to overtake the chariot. Philip would not have known who was in the chariot, but he probably recognized that the occupant was a person of wealth or importance, but he was not intimidated. The chariot may have possibly had an Ethiopian flag or insignia of some sort, since the eunuch worked for the Queen of Ethiopia. To overtake the chariot means the chariot was moving, not parked or sitting still. Philip ran to the chariot and heard the eunuch reading the prophet Isaiah. In those days whenever people read, they did so out loud.

THE EUNUCH WAS ACTUALLY READING ABOUT THE DEATH OF JESUS

At the very moment that Philip approached the Ethiopian eunuch, the eunuch was reading Isaiah 53:7-8 out loud. This was a portion of Isaiah's prophetic word about Jesus death on the cross. It is a focus on Jesus' death on the cross, but unbeknownst to the eunuch, the death of Jesus on the cross impacted the death of all humanity, including his own eventual death.

Isaiah 53:7-8 "He was oppressed and He was afflicted. Yet He opened not His mouth; He was led as a sheep to the slaughter, and a sheep before its shearer is silent. So He opened not His mouth. He was taken from prison and from judgment, And who will declare His generation? For He was cut off from the land of the living; For the transgressions of My people He was stricken".

IN THE 1st CENTURY OR 21st CENTURY FEAR OF COMING DEATH IS THE BIBLICAL KEY TO WIN SOULS

Isaiah 53, focuses on the sacrificial death of Jesus Christ on the cross and what He accomplished on the cross. Philip knew exactly what the eunuch was reading. Philip would have been very experienced at presenting the salvation gospel of Jesus Christ by using the 53rd chapter of Isaiah. Philip's question "Do you understand what you are reading" was strategized. He developed it to create teachable moments when he presented Christ to Jews. He would have been used to asking this same question or a variation of it from many previous encounters.

The strategy in Philip's question was to raise a question and concern in the eunuch's mind about death and in particular the death of the man he was reading about, whose death would impact the eunuch's own coming death. (To create teachable moments, Philip would have been very experienced at asking Jews if they understood what the prophet Isaiah meant about the death of the man in what is in the bible as the 53rd chapter of Isaiah. This strategy was how Philip created a desire in Jews to want to hear the salvation gospel, to then lead or win them to Christ.) Philip used a variation of this same strategy around the subject of death, to instantly create a concern and interest in the eunuch that there was something for him to understand far beyond what he just read.

IN PERSONAL EVANGELISM PHILIP WAS STRATEGICALLY MINDED

Philip was experienced in leading unsaved Jews to accept Jesus as their Savior in personal evangelism. Philip developed and had a strategized salvation gospel presentation, which would create a teachable moment in order to present or preach Christ. He could have easily had and probably did have a copy of Isaiah that he carried to show to unsaved Jews. He perhaps asked them to read it and then ask his strategic question "Do you understand what you are reading?" in order to create a teachable moment for him to then present Christ.

In Acts 8:32-33, the teachable moment Philip created with his strategic question was where the eunuch was reading about the death of a man. Unknown to the eunuch, the man was Jesus Christ and His work on the cross. Philip's strategic question "Do you understand what you are reading?" was to create a desire in the eunuch to want to hear more and then preach or present Christ. To preach or present Christ with this salvation gospel presentation mean the same thing, because they both refer to being structured and strategized.

In presenting Christ, Philip would have taught how the death of Jesus on the cross would impact the future death of the eunuch as he led the Ethiopian eunuch to accept Jesus as his Savior. This was not in a church or on a building platform. It was personal evangelism on a chariot/wagon seat.

Philip had a prepared strategy for what he wanted to do in his personal evangelism. This is why Philip is the biblical personal evangelism role model to lead or win any unsaved person to Christ and what the biblically strategized salvation gospel presentation will prepare you to do.

ALL UNSAVED PEOPLE WANT ANSWERS ABOUT DEATH

At that moment, because of the eunuch's concern and interest around the death of the man in the scripture, Philip's strategic question created an instant desire in the eunuch to want answers about death. The eunuch had no idea that he was actually reading about his own coming death, because the death of the man in the scripture impacted his own coming death.

The eunuch would not have understood it, but his desire for answers about death was his instant willingness and desire to want to hear the salvation gospel of Jesus Christ. Upon hearing the salvation gospel presentation from Philip, which gave him the biblical answer to his own coming death, the eunuch accepted Jesus as his Savior. Any unsaved person can be stimulated to instantly have a concern and a desire to want to hear answers about their own coming death, just like the eunuch did, which is what this salvation gospel presentation will do. This gospel presentation will instantly create a desire in any unsaved person to want to hear the salvation gospel exactly the same way as the biblical model, to then lead or win the unsaved person to their decision for Christ.

The eunuch not only did not understand who the man was in the text, but had no idea what was spiritually taking place with the death of the man. Before Philip encountered him, all the eunuch knew or understood, was that he was reading about a man's death in a scripture. It was Philip's strategic question that got the eunuch's attention and instantly created the desire for the eunuch to want to hear answers about the man and death. The eunuch is the role model for all unsaved people who have little to no understanding about what biblically takes place at death. All unsaved people want answers about death and most particularly their own coming death.

WHY PHILIP IS THE PERSONAL EVANGELISM ROLE MODEL

Do you think it was an accident or coincidence that as Philip approached the eunuch, the eunuch was reading about the prophetic death of Jesus? This encounter was no accident or coincidence. It was a uniquely timed encounter that was purposely orchestrated by the Spirit of God. This Spirit led encounter highlights that Philip is the biblical personal evangelism role model. It underscores the need to be prepared to introduce the coming death of unsaved people. In personal evangelism to know how to gently introduce the coming death of an unsaved person is extremely important. The bible is teaching how to do personal evangelism using Philip as the role model. He is the example of the need to be led by the Spirit in order to know who to present the strategized salvation gospel presentation to and when to present it, Philip was led by the Spirit to the eunuch. He is the only individual in the bible that intentionally and strategically led an unsaved person to a decision to accept Jesus as their Savior. Philip's Spirit led strategized salvation gospel presentation for personal evangelism is the only biblical model and way to consistently introduce, present and conclude the salvation gospel with an immediate salvation result. This is what the biblically strategized salvation gospel presentation will do for you, why Philip is the personal evangelism role model and this book is entitled WHAT TO SAY EVANGELISM.

PHILIP MAY HAVE INCLUDED OTHER PROPHETIC WORDS ABOUT JESUS CHRIST

In the process of leading the eunuch to his decision for Christ, Philip may have possibly referred the eunuch to two other prophetic verses from Isaiah and one from Micah.

Isaiah 7: 14 "Therefore the Lord Himself will give you a sign: Behold, the virgin shall conceive and bear a Son, and shall call His name Immanuel"

Isaiah 9:6-7 "For unto us a Child is born, Unto us a Son is given; And the government will be upon His shoulder. And His name will be called Wonderful, Counselor, Mighty God, Everlasting Father, Prince of Peace. Of the increase of His government and peace There will be no end, Upon the throne of David and over His kingdom, To order it and establish it with judgement and justice from that time forward, even Forever."

Micah 5:2"But you Bethlehem Ephrathah, though you are little among the thousands of Judah, Yet out of you shall come forth to Me The One to be Ruler in Israel, Whose goings forth are from of old, From everlasting."

It is possible that Philip presented and explained these scriptures, because he would have been quite familiar with them. The eunuch had a Torah or a copy of Isaiah, was reading Isaiah and may have had a question about them.

CHAPTER TWELVE

THE NON RELATIONSHIP LESSON IN THE PHILIP AND EUNUCH ENCOUNTER

The bible is clearly teaching that the idealistically promoted requirement to have a deep or meaningful relationship with unsaved people as the key to leading them to a decision for Christ is simply, not true. The relational lesson of Philip and the eunuch is that no relationship at all is necessary to actually lead an unsaved person to Christ. What the bible actually demonstrates and teaches is that what Christians need to know is "what to say and why to say it, who to say it to, when to say it, where to say it and how to say it" to lead any unsaved person to Christ in any situation or depth of any relationship.

DO VISITORS KNOW THE SPEAKER THAT GIVES AN INVITATION TO RECEIVE CHRIST

Have you ever been in a church or crusade type service and the speaker gives an invitation or appeal to those who are unsaved to come forward to receive Christ? They may give an invitation to come forward, to look up or raise a hand as a sign that they are receiving or accepting Christ. What is the relationship between the speaker and the unsaved person in the audience or congregation, that they have never met? The answer is none, because there is no relationship at any level. An unsaved visitor may have a sense of safety about the speaker from just being in a church. Whenever unsaved people visit a church, they do not have a relationship with the speaker. When unsaved people visit a church, they have made themselves available to hear a salvation gospel presentation. The biblically strategized salvation gospel presentation will instantly create a desire in unsaved people to want to hear the salvation gospel of Jesus Christ. Keep in mind that 95% to 100% of your unsaved family members and friends who hear it will accept Jesus Christ as their Savior.

RELATIONSHIPS ARE IMPORTANT BUT NOT KEY TO LEAD OR WIN AN UNSAVED PERSON TO CHRIST

Please, do not misunderstand, I am certainly not against building relationships with unsaved people. Every Christian is always in a relationship with unsaved people at one level or another. The reality and priority is that irrespective of the depth of a relationship between a Christian and an unsaved person, a Christian must be prepared at all times to know what to say in order to lead any unsaved person to Christ. The ultimate evangelism value of a relationship or ongoing rapport is ongoing accessibility to at the right time lead an unsaved person to Christ. Every year all over the world millions of unsaved people die and will go to hell. In America untold numbers of unsaved people die every year. They all die in contact with or were in some level of relationship with probably hundreds of Christians who simply did not know how to lead them to Christ.

ONLY THE HOLY SPIRIT KNOWS EVERYTHING ABOUT PEOPLE SAVED OR UNSAVED

It is only the Holy Spirit who knows how vulnerable or available any unsaved person is at any given time. All unsaved people have made mistakes in life, done wrong things and they all know it. All unsaved people want answers to life issues, but in particular, answers about death. They all want Jesus as their Savior, whether they consciously know it or not. Unsaved people do not realize they are being drawn by the Spirt of the Lord to Jesus Christ. They are being drawn to Him and you are being drawn to them in order to present this one of a kind salvation gospel presentation. Jn 12:32 "And I, if I am lifted up from the earth, will draw all peoples to Myself." He does this through the power of the Holy Spirit.

IF YOUR CHURCH WON'T WIN TO CHRIST
THEN YOU BETTER LEARN HOW TO DO IT

If you are part of a church that has a little or no evangelism emphasis and you have unsaved family and friends, you should have and need to have a concern about their salvation. If you do have salvation concerns about unsaved family and friends, then it will be up to you to learn how to lead them to Christ. It is always a good idea to invite an unsaved person to church, but if there is no evangelistic emphasis, you better learn how to win them to Christ. It is far better to first lead an unsaved person to Christ and to then invite them to church as a new Christian or refer them to another church. This all comes down to you realizing that you need to learn how to lead or win unsaved family members and friends to Christ yourself with the biblically strategized salvation gospel presentation.

ALL UNSAVED PEOPLE FEAR COMING DEATH

All unsaved people share the same common denominator and specific reason to want salvation in Christ, which is from their unspoken fear of death. After you learn this gospel presentation, you will be prepared to lead any unsaved person to Christ. This includes unsaved family and friends when the Holy Spirt or an Angel of the Lord leads you or "prompts you" to present it to a specific unsaved person. The role of witnessing Christians is to know how to lead an unsaved person to Christ, not to analyze them or try and be the Holy Spirt in an unsaved person's life. Trying to "convict unsaved people" by criticizing or condemning them will drive unsaved people away from the Lord, not draw them to the Lord.

John 14:16 "And I will pray the Father, and he will give you another Helper, that He may abide with you forever."

HOW TO KNOW WHEN THE HOLY SPIRIT IS LEADING YOU

Some Christians may ask "How will I know the Holy Spirit wants me to now present the biblically strategized salvation gospel to an unsaved person? How will I know when He is leading me?" The answer is you may suddenly "feel an irresistible urge to present the biblically strategized salvation gospel presentation to a particular person." You may feel "drawn to present it to a particular person." It could be a man, woman, boy or girl. To be compelled or to feel compelled means to sense a strong, irresistible urge to do a particular thing. In an evangelism scenario, it is feeling "a strong urge" to present this salvation gospel to a particular unsaved person. A witnessing Christian may have the thought or feeling of "I can't stop myself, I have to present this salvation gospel presentation to this person." This is what being led, prompted or impressed by the Holy Spirit or an Angel of the Lord, can feel like and to know when to present the salvation gospel presentation. This is what I sense and feel when the Lord wants me to present this gospel presentation. When you sense or feel an urge to present this gospel presentation, assume by faith it is of the Lord and present it.

NOW FREE TO SENSE THE LEADING OF THE HOLY SPIRIT

When you learn the biblically strategized salvation gospel presentation. You will know what to say and do when interacting with any unsaved person. You will feel and know a new kind of freedom. This freedom is a freedom from the fear and uncertainty of not knowing what to say and how to interact evangelistically with unsaved people. It is this freedom that will free you to have a clear sense of when the Holy Spirit or an Angel of the Lord is ministering to you in order for you to minister this gospel presentation to an unsaved person.

CHRISTIANS ARE HIS REPRESENTATIVE
AND REPRESENTATION

All individual members of the body of Christ, both men and women are His representatives and representation, a witness to Him. He is ministering through witnessing Christians that know how to lead or win unsaved people to Him. You as a man or woman of God in Jesus Christ, are the body of Christ. Christians are literally His body, because after His death, burial, resurrection and ascension to heaven, His physical body was no longer on the earth. His physical body today is the body of Christ to represent Him and to do God's will in His name to fulfill the Great Commission.

Acts 1:8 "But you shall receive power when the Holy Spirit has come upon you; and you shall be witnesses to Me in Jerusalem, and in all Judea and Samaria, and to the end of the earth."

TIME FOR YOU TO LEARN THE BIBLICALLY
STRATEGIZED SALVATION GOSPEL PRESENTATION

I would never suggest that you forget all you have ever heard or learned about personal evangelism. I do suggest that you temporarily set it all aside. First, memorize and learn the biblically strategized salvation gospel presentation. I guarantee you, whomever you are, that the biblically strategized salvation gospel presentation is the answer to what you have been searching for in personal evangelism.

Life is full of distractions, but however they come, do not let them distract you. Learning the biblically strategized salvation gospel presentation is more than just a cute or fun Sunday School exercise. Make the commitment to learn the biblically strategized salvation gospel presentation. When you do, you will go far beyond the historical and traditional generalized personal evangelism mindset. Generalized witnessing is great, but only when men, women and mature teens know how to transition from it into the biblically strategized salvation gospel presentation in order to know how to introduce, present and conclude the salvation gospel with an immediate salvation result.

Do the work, eternal souls are at stake. Second, after you learn it, put all of your previous personal evangelism knowledge in the context of this unique salvation gospel presentation. It will take a little effort and study, but after you learn it, you will have the most powerful personal evangelism tool imaginable! When you present it to unsaved people, they will completely understand why they need to immediately accept and receive Jesus Christ as their own Savior. Thirdly, trust the Lord as you start presenting the biblically strategized salvation gospel presentation and He will be with you. He will not only be with you, but use you, transform you and gloriously bless your life.

One afternoon I was talking with a pastor from another church about personal evangelism. I was sharing my experience about how easy it is to win souls in personal evangelism. Suddenly, he became very emotional and literally broke down in tears as he said to me "I am not afraid to talk to anyone about Jesus, I love to talk to unsaved people about Jesus and getting saved, but "I JUST CAN'T CLOSE THE DEAL!" I taught him the biblically strategized salvation gospel presentation. Prov 11:30b "And he who wins souls is wise."

CHAPTER THIRTEEN

A SKILL THAT CHANGES LIVES FOR ETERNITY BUT ONLY IF YOU LEARN IT

A young lady attended one of my seminars on How to Win Souls in Personal Evangelism. I saw her a few weeks later and she was upset. Her father was unsaved and was divorced from her mother. The father was dating a woman that was part of a false religion and she was very worried about her father. She was upset because she started presenting the gospel presentation and she started the death and danger question by asking "Dad, let me ask you this, when you die and it's time for you to go to heaven and Jesus Christ asks you_____, why should I give you eternal life in heaven? What would you say to Jesus?" She said her father answered and said, I don't know. I have tried to live a good life......She told him, "Dad, that is a normal response for someone like you. I know you have tried to live a good life............At this moment she realized that she was lost in what to say next. She did not have the salvation gospel presentation thoroughly memorized and the process stopped. Her father was prepared to accept Jesus and was ready and willing to be led to Christ, but she had not learned what to say step by step in the gospel presentation. She was upset and heartbroken at herself and for her father. I encourage you to take the time, energy and effort you need, to memorize and learn this unique gospel presentation like you know your own name.

TAKE THE TIME AND EFFORT TO PREPARE YOURSELF FOR THE REST OF YOUR LIFE

The biblically strategized salvation gospel presentation is not hard to learn, but it does have to be learned. Do not short cut your learning process by thinking "all I have to do is familiarize myself with it and I'll just wing it." Make a commitment to the Lord and to yourself that you will make the effort and take the time to seriously learn this salvation gospel presentation. If you do, you will have it and you will lead unsaved people to Christ for the rest of your life.

IS IT ETHICAL OR BIBLICAL TO ASK STRATEGIZED QUESTIONS?

To ask an unsaved person strategic questions in order to prepare them to hear the word of God and truth is not new, it is a time tested biblical tactic. The very first example of asking unsaved people a strategic question to lead or direct them to be reconciled and in right relationship with God took place in the Garden of Eden. It is the story of Adam and Eve after their fall in the Garden of Eden. The Lord God did not approach them to condemn them or yell at them by saying things like; "What have you done! How could you do something so against My will? Do you realize the enormity of what you have done?" He loved His creation and out of His love for them wanted to reach out to gently prepare them for reconciliation.

THE LORD GOD ASKED A STRATEGIC QUESTION

He asked Adam a simple question; "Where are you?" Of course, He knew where both Adam and Eve were physically and spiritually. He gently asked them a strategically framed question to create a teachable moment in order to cause Adam to give an answer for what they had done. His goal was to bring them into accountability for their original sin.

Genesis 3: 8-9 "And they heard the sound of the Lord walking in the garden in the cool of the day, and Adam and his wife hid themselves from the presence of the Lord God among the trees of the garden. Then the Lord God called to Adam and said to him, "Where are you?""

THE LORD GOD DID NOT ASK ADAM
A RANDOM QUESTION

The Lord God asked this particular question in order to position Adam to draw out an answer and account of why he changed his behavior. He created a teachable moment. The Lord God asked him this question in this way to cause Adam to answer for what he and Eve did, in order for him to recognize his responsibility before a loving God. The Lord God established a pattern from the beginning of how to deal with people in sin. The pattern He demonstrated was strategically using a question to create a teachable moment to prepare unsaved people to want to hear the word of God and today, receive Jesus as Savior.

JESUS USED THE SAME STRATEGY TO
REVEAL HIMSELF TO HIS DISCIPLES

In Matthew 16: 13-16, when Jesus knew that this was the right time to reveal the truth of Who He is, He asked two very strategic questions.

"When Jesus came into the region of Caesarea Philippi, He asked His disciples, saying "Who do men say that I, the Son of Man, am?" So they said, "Some say John the Baptist, some Elijah, and others Jeremiah or one of the prophets." He said to them, "But who do you say that I am?" Simon Peter answered and said, "You are the Christ, the Son of the living God."

JESUS ASKED THEM HE DID NOT TELL THEM

First, Jesus asked a strategic question about the general population's belief about Himself. He asked, "Who do men say that I, the Son of Man, am?" His first question prepared them for His second question. Their initial answer was to give Him rumor information. "Some say John the Baptist, some Elijah, and others Jeremiah or one of the prophets." Jesus remained cool, calm and collected. He did not react by demeaning or ridiculing their answer. He patiently let them answer. He asked the first question to lead the disciples to begin thinking about Who He is and to want the answer.

JESUS ALSO ASKED HIS DISCIPLES A STRATEGIC QUESTION

This was to prepare them for the key question directly to them. He asked "But who do you say that I am?" Through these questions He was preparing His disciples to become receptive minded and teachable, so He created a teachable moment. He wanted them to be prepared to hear and to receive the truth about Himself. It was Peter that answered as the Spirit led him. Peter declared "You are the Christ, the Son of the living God." Jesus prepared the disciples to become receptive to hear the answer that Jesus knew was coming. He strategically asked two questions to create a teachable moment.

JESUS COULD HAVE SIMPLY TOLD THEM BUT HE DID NOT FOR A REASON

Jesus could have simply told them who He is, by telling them "Men, gather around, I have an announcement about who I, the

Son of man, am. Men, don't listen to rumors, I am the Christ, the Son of the living God." He did not do that, He prepared them to want to hear, in order to receive what He knew Peter would tell them. Jesus Christ, Himself is demonstrating the power of strategically asking questions to create a teachable moment in order to prepare people to receive truth. To create a teachable moment is an intentional act. It is not a random or accidental event. To create a teachable moment is an intentional event with a purpose. For our purposes, creating a teachable moment is by instantly preparing unsaved people to want to hear answers about their eventual death and the salvation gospel of Jesus Christ.

ASKING QUESTIONS TO PREPARE PEOPLE TO WANT TO HEAR ANSWERS

Jesus prepared His disciples to hear in order to be ready to receive, which is vastly different from just telling people information without preparing them to want to hear it. This is what makes all the difference in witnessing with no goal, direction, structure or strategy and presenting the strategized salvation gospel in order to create a teachable moment. Jesus and Philip used the same strategy. They had different conversations, but their strategy was the same. This one of a kind salvation gospel presentation has the same strategy.

THE UNSAVED WORLD KNOWS THE VALUE OF ASKING QUESTIONS

Socrates 469-399bc, is considered to be the greatest secular teacher of history. He was known for teaching his classes by asking his students questions that they struggled with and this gave him the opportunity to direct them to what he wanted teach them. In colleges and universities this is known as the Socratic Teaching Method.

CHAPTER FOURTEEN

LEAD THEM TO CHRIST PRAY FOR THEM INVITE OR ENCOURAGE THEM TO CHURCH

After the conclusion and the unsaved person has been led to their decision for Christ offer to pray for them. They will welcome your prayer of blessing for them, their family and whatever need they may have shared about with you. If they are a family member or friend in the same community invite them to your church or refer them to another church in the area where they live. If you don't know of a local church for them, offer to help them find one. If you lead an unsaved person to Christ on the telephone do the same thing to help them find a church.

HOW TO INTRODUCE THE SALVATION GOSPEL ON THE TELEPHONE

If you have concerns or have been praying about an unsaved family member or friend, it is easy to lead or win them to Christ. Pray and ask the Lord for the right time to call to lead them to Christ. The right time can come at any time, but when you sense the right time, make the call. When you call, talk about whatever is appropriate and at the right time, start the gospel presentation. They may already know that you are a Christian or they may not know you are a Christian. Learn this strategized salvation gospel presentation and make the call.

IF OLD FRIENDS DO NOT KNOW YOU ARE A CHRISTIAN TODAY TELL THEM

If you have not spoken with the person you are calling in a while, take the time to share where you are in life and that you accepted Jesus as your Savior. If they do not know that you have become a Christian, you can say something like this at the appropriate time. **Say To Them:**

"I accepted Jesus as my Savior and became a Christian and I do evangelism work. This means I talk to people about Jesus Christ, salvation and eternal life, things like that. May I ask you a question without being to personal?" Let them say **"Yes"** and continue the gospel presentation.

If they already know that you are a Christian, you say: **"As you know I have been a Christian for a while and now I do evangelism work. This means I talk to people about Jesus Christ, salvation and eternal life. May I ask you a question without being to personal?"** Let them say **"Yes"** and continue the presentation.

It is simple to shift the conversation into introducing the biblically strategized salvation gospel presentation. What is important for you, a witnessing Christian, is to learn this salvation gospel presentation as well as you know your own address and telephone number. It is not hard to lead an unsaved person to Christ on the telephone and there may be people from your past that you have concerns about and so I encourage you to pray for them, call them up and lead them to Christ.

WHAT TO SAY AND DO IF THERE IS MORE THAN ONE UNSAVED PERSON

A situation that witnessing Christians may possibly find themselves is presenting the biblically strategized salvation gospel presentation to more than one person at a time. It could be two, three or four people at the same time. It does not matter, because if the Lord has led you to lead or win them all to Christ, you absolutely will! The only variation is at the end when you say "Let me ask you this, would you like to know that you can have eternal life in heaven someday?"

At this moment make sure you get a "Yes" from each individual before you say "Okay, I'd like to lead you in a short prayer. This will be your prayer. We are going to invite Jesus Christ to be your Savior, forgive you of your sins and give you eternal life. I will lead the prayer, you repeat the prayer. Will you pray with me?" Again, get a "yes" from each individual before you say "This is your prayer, I will lead the prayer, you repeat the prayer: Heavenly Father, I accept Jesus Christ as my Savior. I ask you to forgive me of my sins and give me eternal life and I will seek your will for my life. In Jesus name I pray, Amen." If there are several unsaved people, they will all follow you and will pray to receive Him as Savior. I have done this many times over the years.

WITNESSING OR SOWING WITHOUT REAPING IS ALWAYS DANGEROUS

Generally, witnessing is about laying ground work for possibly another evangelism event. To witness and get people interested in spiritual or Godly things and to not actually complete the witnessing process by leading them to a decision for Christ is extremely dangerous. It is dangerous, because Satan is harvesting souls through a host of cults, psychic's, New Age false religions including exotic sounding Eastern religions. The broad "self- help" teachings have many enslaved in the worship of "self." Satan, through his network of false religions, preys on the curious, but uninformed and unsaved people of the world.

MANY UNSAVED PEOPLE BELIEVE
THAT GOD NO LONGER EXISTS

A very contemporary deceptive religious concept that targets uninformed and unsaved people is a type of religious belief called Pandeism. This word is a combination of Pantheism and Deism. Pantheism promotes that God is in everything. Deism means that God is somehow no longer involved with His creation. This false religious view is why many have come to believe that God, the Creator of the universe, no longer exists, because He became the universe and is now the universe. Many unsaved people believe that the universe makes decisions about people.

MANY ARE BEING DECEIVED AND HARVESTED
BY SATAN AND THE WORLD

They believe that God has ceased to exist and became what He created and so it is now the universe that is making decisions for humanity. I actually overheard a successful attorney once comment that "a problem was solved by the universe". This false religious view is promoted in many movies and television that the youth of the world watch. The intended message is "the universe makes this happen." In movies, the subliminal message is when audiences generally see an unusual gathering of "storm clouds with lightning flashes", to emphasize a dramatic transformative signaling event. This is the "dramatic subliminal sign" for viewers to believe that it is the universe that is influencing mankind and making things happen.

YOUNG PEOPLE MUST BE WON TO
CHRIST AS SOON AS POSSIBLE

The danger in generalized witnessing to young people with no decision for Christ is that all unsaved people want Jesus Christ, they just don't know it yet. Young people can easily be led into a false, but attractive sounding substitute. Uninformed and unsaved people of all ages are susceptible to deceitful religious philosophies. This is because they may think all things "spiritual sounding" contain a moral or spiritual equivalence. They don't understand themselves what they really want and Satan and the world will convince them that their lies and false religions are the truth. Satan and the world are ready to harvest the unsaved, that the body of Christ does not know how to harvest. When Satan wins an unsaved person into a false religion of any kind, he has tightened his grip on them.

VERY YOUNG PEOPLE ARE EASY TO LEAD TO CHRIST

Young people as young as four, five years of age, are easy to lead to decisions for Christ. One of the significant reasons that they are so easy to lead to Christ, besides being so trusting, is that this gospel presentation is easily understood, non -threatening and non-critical. Young people are extremely sensitive about being criticized. A powerful quality of this strategized salvation gospel presentation is that it is completely void of any form of criticism. It was developed to eliminate any criticism of unsaved people. Even young people as young a four and five years of age will completely understand everything you gently present to them with this gospel presentation. Children understand and always receive Jesus as their Savior. If you are a parent or grandparent do not hesitate to present this salvation gospel presentation to your young family members and their friends.

BE WILLING TO HUMBLE YOURSELF

If there are unsaved people that you have argued with or feel the door is closed to win them to Christ, re-open that door. The way to do that is to pray and ask or the Lord's leading on the matter and as He leads, then reach out to them. Reach out or contact them and apologize to them for being part of an argument and possibly offending them. It doesn't matter who was at fault. What is important is that they understand that you are willing to reach out to them. If this is your unsaved family member or friend be willing to humble yourself and give yourself an opportunity to lead them to Christ. Reopen the relationship as best you can and as the Holy Spirit leads, no matter who they are or where they live and at the appropriate time gently introduce the biblically strategized salvation gospel presentation. Always pray and the Lord will be with you and the other person. The opportunity to lead them to Christ may not happen on the first call, but if you reopen the relational door, pray for the right time and it will happen eventually.

A PASTOR LEARNED HOW TO LEAD
HIS BROTHER TO CHRIST

A pastor once hosted one of my seminars on how to win souls in personal evangelism. At the end of the seminar, I asked if there was anyone who had an unsaved family member or friend that they had been witnessing to and I said I would call them on my cell phone and lead them to Christ. The seminar was over, the pastor told people that they could leave, but they all stayed to see how this was going to happen. They wanted to see if leading unsaved people to Christ on the telephone could be done with this gospel presentation. To say they were curious is an understatement. One of the women gave me the name and telephone number of a man she had been witnessing to and I called him, you could have heard a pin drop as I led him to Christ. I did so with the same biblically strategized salvation gospel presentation that you are going to learn.

THIS PASTOR WANTED TO LEARN HOW TO WIN SOULS AND HE DID

A few weeks later I saw the pastor and he told me that he had a brother dying from cancer, that for many years he had been praying for and witnessing to him. He said that he presented the biblically strategized salvation gospel to him and his brother received the Lord. All Christians, clergy and non-clergy alike, can now learn how to win souls in personal evangelism, irrespective of their gender, title, office status or stature.

If you are a Pastor, this is a golden opportunity to let those in your congregation get equipped to learn how to win souls in personal evangelism. Every Christian has unsaved family members, friends and they all encounter unsaved strangers. This is an opportunity to let a personal evangelism ministry develop, see unsaved people won to Christ then invited to your church, see church growth and a fresh evangelistic excitement in your church. The vision of this personal evangelism ministry is to create a paradigm shift away from traditional personal evangelism thinking that has completely shut down most Christians. It is estimated that around 95% of all Christians have never led a single unsaved person to Christ. These numbers have been around for at least the last fifty years. Whatever the precise numbers may be, there are untold millions of Christians who have no idea how to lead any unsaved person to Jesus as Savior. This training can reverse these high numbers that represent Christians in all churches who are not equipped or prepared to win souls in personal evangelism.

Eph 4:11-12 "And He Himself gave some to be apostles, some prophets, some evangelists, and some pastors and teachers, for the equipping of the saints for the work of the ministry, for the edifying of the body of Christ."

CHAPTER FIFTEEN

FIRST WIN THEN INVITE THEN DISCIPLE THEN EQUIP IS EVANGELISM W.I.D.E.

The overarching goal is to create a fresh personal evangelism mindset and model, based upon men, women and mature teens actually learning how to lead unsaved people to Christ. This overarching goal and attitude is to lead or win any unsaved person to Christ and to then invite them or bring them to your local church as new believers in Jesus Christ. The second part of the Great Commission is to teach them, which is discipleship and this is best done in a bible believing church or a bible believing home group of some sort that is connected to a church. Christians are used to inviting unsaved family members and friends to visit their church to hopefully be led to Christ by another "perceived more qualified person."

A FRESH VIEW OF WHEN TO INVITE TO CHURCH

This teaching is to train and equip Christians how to lead unsaved people to their decisions for Christ in personal evangelism and develop a fresh mindset about church visitation. This new mindset is to win them to Christ first and then invite them to church. After you learn this gospel presentation, you will quickly discover that in the 21st Century, it is much easier to lead an unsaved person to Christ than it is to invite an unsaved person to church and actually get them to the church. It is best to first lead them to Christ and to then invite or bring them to church as a new Christian.

EVANGELISM W.I.D.E. MEANS TO
WIN INVITE DISCIPLE EQUIP

The goal of this book is to teach every Christian man, woman and mature teen exactly how to be prepared to lead or win any unsaved person to Christ. With this new fresh ability, you will also have a new perspective on church invitation. The term win is from the Apostle Paul in 1Cor9:19, when he describes to win an unsaved person to Christ, is like being in a contest. EVANGELISM W.I.D.E. stands for W, "Win" them to Christ first. I, stands for "Invite" them to your church or bible fellowship after you have won them to Christ. D, stands for after you have won them, they are invited to church or bible fellowship to be "Discipled". E, stands for "Equip". Every Christian needs to be discipled and equipped to do the work of the ministry, which should include being trained on how to lead or win unsaved people to Christ.

EVANGELISM W.I.D.E. IS THE ULTIMATE
PERSONAL EVANGELISM GAME CHANGER

In personal evangelism, a Christian involved in general witnessing or a general conversation on any subject with an unsaved person, now has the ability to change, transition or shift into the biblically strategized salvation gospel presentation. In doing so, be prepared to immediately lead an unsaved person to their decision to accept Jesus as their own Savior.

The traditional personal evangelism world view has been to "witness to invite" to Christian events with the hope of an eventual salvation, irrespective if it is to visit a church, bible study, cell group or crusade. With this salvation gospel presentation, it is now far easier to win the unsaved to Christ than to invite the unsaved to church and actually get them to church.

Evangelism W.I.D.E. in the 21st century, because of the biblically strategized salvation gospel presentation, represents the opportunity for a complete personal evangelism paradigm shift. It represents a new personal evangelism outreach thought process to fulfill the Great Commission.

It is the evangelistic way forward for the body of Christ in the midst of a globally and politically aggressive anti-Christ culture.

BE SALT AND LIGHT & AS POLITE AS YOU CAN BE

If you are part of a church and would like to develop an area evangelism outreach, I suggest that you first learn the biblically strategized salvation gospel presentation for your own use, no matter where you happen to be. Ask your Pastor for permission and discuss outreach ideas with the Pastor. A simple suggestion that works, is to map out an area around the local church as the mission field. Develop a brochure or something as simple as a flyer that identifies the church, the Pastor and location. If appropriate have some church cards printed and perhaps a contact card for yourself. This and a notepad to write down names and addresses of new contacts, is all you need to start.

WHEN YOU KNOCK ON A DOOR

Have your brochure or flyer and personal note pad and simply knock on a door. Let me assure you, no one is going to "bite your head off or throw rocks at you." People are generally polite. Stand a few feet away from the door and if there are two of you do not stand side by side, but one behind the other. It is best to go in pairs, but men can go alone, but women should not go alone.

At the door introduce yourself and say the following. This is only a suggestion of what to say at the door. Certainly, feel free to develop whatever you want to say, but this is simple and effective. Unsaved people like simple and to the point.

"Hi, my name is "your name" and I am part of "your church name" that is not far from here and we wanted to stop by and leave you this brochure/flyer to let you know about our church, everyone is welcome and to let you know that we pray for you and all of your neighbors. The reason we stopped by is we also wanted to know if you have any specific prayer requests that we can pray about for you and your family? (do not ask if you can come inside their home. If they invite you in, fine. Do not appear intrusive or threatening at any level. This is a neighborly drop by type visit, so keep it low key) We are Christians and we do evangelism work. This means we talk to people about Jesus Christ, salvation and eternal life, things like that. May I ask you a question without being to personal?.........and continue on with the biblically strategized salvation gospel presentation. Lead them to Jesus as their Savior and then invite them to your church. It is that simple.

WHAT TO SAY AND DO IF YOU ARE LED TO LEAD A STRANGER TO CHRIST

One afternoon I was in a supermarket in the vegetable department and a woman I had never met and I started talking about vegetables. I don't remember exactly how the conversation started, I think there was a sale of some kind, but I felt led to present the salvation gospel presentation to her. I had already introduced myself and told her my name and she told me her name.

I said, "I am a Christian and I do evangelism work. This means I talk to a lot of people about Jesus Christ, salvation and eternal life, things like that. May I ask you a question

without being to personal" She said, "Yes." I said, "You know we are all going to die someday, right?" Again, she said "Yes."

I then led her through the very same biblically strategized salvation gospel presentation and at the end she prayed to accept Jesus as her Savior. This took place in the vegetable department in a supermarket as people were walking around us. I did not speak loudly, just above a whisper. No one around us had any idea what we were discussing. Use wisdom as you present Christ to unsaved people, no matter where you happened to be. She became a member of our church for twelve years before she moved out of state.

TO WALK UP TO A STRANGER

You may be anywhere in public and suddenly feel led to approach a stranger. When you do, know that the Holy Spirit or an Angel of the Lord is letting you know that the stranger, irrespective if they are a man, woman, boy or girl, is available to hear the salvation gospel presentation. Simply approach the stranger, introduce yourself, tell them you are a Christian, that you do evangelism work and say, may I ask you a question without being to personal? When you state that you "are a Christian and do evangelism work" there is an immediate "raised level" of respect for you. It is literally that simple.

IF YOU HAVE AN OPPORTUNITY TO WIN
A JEWISH PERSON TO CHRIST

Over the years I have led many Jewish people to decisions for Jesus Christ with the biblically strategized salvation gospel presentation except for one additional insert. When you finish explaining the second part of Romans 6:23, you insert the following;

"Joe, the second half of that scripture says 'but the gift of God is eternal life through Jesus Christ our Lord.' What that means is when Jesus was here on the earth, He went to the cross and took upon Himself the sin of the world. He died, was buried and the third day He arose from the dead and later ascended to Heaven. When Moses was on the earth, he brought the Law and the sacrifice of bulls and lambs with the shedding of their blood to make atonement for sin. Animal sacrifice for sin ended when Jesus Christ died on the cross, was buried and rose again. His shed blood washed away sin. Jesus said 'I came for the Jew first and I did not come to destroy the law, but to fulfill the law.' "Joe, if we accept Jesus' sacrifice on the cross for our own sins, our sins are forgiven, and when we die. we can have eternal life in Heaven." Now continue on to the conclusion and lead the unsaved Jewish person in the prayer to accept Jesus as their Savior.

JEWS NEED TO KNOW THERE IS NO ATONEMENT FROM ANIMAL SACRIFICE

The insert is specifically for Jewish people to hear and understand that with the coming of Jesus Christ, the Lord God stopped making atonement for the sins of Jews with the sacrifice of bulls and lambs. The sins of all, both Jew and Gentile alike are forgiven by faith in Jesus Christ and his sacrifice for sins on the cross. All Christians should be aware of Romans 1:16

"For I am not ashamed of the gospel of Christ, for it is the power of God to salvation for everyone who believes, for the Jew first and also for the Greek."

The other scripture to be familiar with is Matthew 5:17 "Do not think that I came to destroy the Law or the Prophets. I did not come to destroy but to fulfill."

JEWS WILL ACCEPT JESUS AS THEIR SAVIOR AND THE LORD WILL BLESS YOU

Jewish people will relate to and appreciate what you are telling them and will accept Jesus as their Savior. Most Jewish people are not bible scholars and know little about the bible. Jews are God's uniquely chosen people and <u>the Lord God promised to bless those, who bless them.</u>

JEWS ARE GOD'S CHOSEN PEOPLE FOR A REASON

Jews are God's chosen people, because He created and chose them to be witnesses to the world about Himself and for Jesus Christ to come into the world through them. He is Almighty God, Creator of Heaven and Earth and the God of Abraham, Isaac and Jacob. Abraham was a Gentile and the man that God used to begin the family line that became the Nation of Israel and Jews.

The Nation of Israel did not exist until Abraham's grandson Jacob and his name was changed to Israel and he had sons that became the heads of the twelve tribes. When Jacob wrestled with the Lord, He changed Jacob's name to Israel. Gen 32: 28 "And He said, "Your name shall no longer be called Jacob, but Israel; for you have struggled with God and with men, and have prevailed." It is through Jacob, now named Israel that God created the Nation of Israel.

God revealed Himself to the world through the Nation of Israel. The books of Exodus and Deuteronomy show us that He did this by revealing and demonstrating His glorious presence, love and miraculous power with the Ten Plagues, pillars of cloud by day, fire by night and the parting of the Red Sea as He led them out of slavery in Egypt. In the desert, He further revealed and demonstrated His presence, love and the power of His provision with Manna, Quail, and unworn clothes and sandals for 40 years.

At Mount Sinai He uniquely revealed His glorious presence and character and the high standard for right living that He had for the Nation of Israel and ultimately the world in Jesus Christ, through the Ten Commandments and the Law. He also revealed His presence in the Tabernacle which means "dwelling place." At that time the Tabernacle was a portable tent for the presence of God as a place of worship as the Nation of Israel moved from place to place. This was before Solomon built the Temple and God dwelled there in the Holy of Holies, on the Ark of the Covenant.

THE NEW COVENANT IN CHRIST WAS FOR JEWS

The New Covenant that God has through Jesus Christ' sacrifice on the cross was for Jews, because they broke His Covenant at Mount Sinai. The New Covenant was prophesied by the Prophet Jeremiah as recorded in Jeremiah 31:31-32 "Behold, the days will come, says the LORD, that I will make a New Covenant with the House of Judah: Not according to the Covenant that I made with their fathers in the day that I took them by the hand to bring them out of the land of Egypt; which My Covenant they broke, although I was an husband unto them, says the LORD." The (KJV) text from Jeremiah is the best translation of the prophetic word that explains why God Almighty was going to create a New Covenant, which was going to be in Jesus Christ.

JESUS INTRODUCED THE NEW COVENANT IN HIMSELF

Jesus Christ Himself, declared and introduced the New Covenant at the Last Supper in Lk 22:19-20 "And He took bread, gave thanks and broke it, and gave it to them, saying, "This is My body which is given for you, do this in remembrance of Me." Likewise He also took the cup after supper, saying, "This cup is the new covenant in My blood, which is shed for you."

Jesus' sacrifice on the cross is the ultimate fulfillment of God's Covenant promise with Abram, who was renamed Abraham. Gen 17:5 "No longer shall your name be called Abram, but your name shall be Abraham; for I have made you a father of many nations."

After Jesus was crucified on Passover, 50 days later came the Day of Pentecost. On that day the Holy Spirit was poured out on Christians to be filled with the Holy Spirt to be anointed, empowered and led by Him. Up until that day the Holy Spirit only came upon Prophets, Priests and Kings. On the Day of Pentecost God changed who He would come upon and where He would dwell.

The Spirt of God was no longer limited to the Ark of the Covenant, dwelling inside a Temple of stone and wood or to only come upon a select few men. The Holy Spirit would now fill men, women, boys and girls when they accept Jesus Christ as their Savior and their sins are forgiven. Christians filled with the Holy Spirit are now His Temple. 1 Cor 6:19 "Or do you not know that your body is the temple of the Holy Spirit who is in you, whom you have from God, and you are not your own?"

CHRISTIAN GENTILES ARE GRAFTED
INTO THE COVENANT PROMISE

The Apostle Paul wrote in Rom 11: 16-17 "For if the firstfruit is holy, the lump is also holy; and if the root is holy, so are the branches. And if some of the branches were broken off, and you, being a wild olive tree, were grafted in among them, and with them became a partaker of the root and fatness of the olive tree," The Lord, through His love for the world, has graciously given the world the opportunity to be saved in Christ and grafted in to the Nation of Israel in order to also become an heir of His promise to Abraham. Gal 3:29 "And if you are Christ's, then you are Abraham's seed, and heirs according to the promise."

Christians can now be equipped and prepared to lead or win Jews to Christ whenever an opportunity presents itself as the Holy Spirt or an Angel leads you to win them. Jews are always a priority with God. Rom 1:16 "For I am not ashamed of the gospel of Christ, for it is the power of God to salvation for everyone who believes, for the Jew first and also for the Greek." (Greek, refers to all Gentiles, irrespective of race or ethnic background.)

The Apostle Paul in Rom 11:1 tell us that God has not cast away His people. "I say then, has God cast away His people? Certainly not! I also am an Israelite, of the seed of Abraham, of the tribe of Benjamin." In Rom 11: 26-27 he further states "and so all Israel will be saved, as it is written: The Deliverer will come out of Zion, And He will turn away ungodliness form Jacob; For this is my covenant with them, When I take away their sins." The Apostle Paul is not saying every Jew will be saved, but there will be a huge group of Jews that will come to Christ.

I included this segment identifying why Jews are God's Chosen People and about the New Covenant to prayerfully and hopefully help familiarize and expand general knowledge about Jewish history. To help equip and expand biblical thinking about Jews in case there are times when you may have an extended conversation with a Jewish person. My hope is to also help transform any negative attitudes about Jews into positive attitudes about Jews and to encourage Christians to not be intimidated about winning Jews to Christ. Christians can now learn how to lead or win unsaved Jews to Christ with the biblically strategized salvation gospel presentation. The body Christ of Christ should wisely support and bless Jews and the Nation of Israel in order to above all, to be in His will and to receive His blessings.

Gen 12:1-3 Now the Lord said to Abram. "Get out of your country, From your family And from your Fathers "house, to a land that I will show you. I will make you a great nation, I will bless you and make your name great; And you shall be a blessing. I will bless those who bless you, And I will curse him who curses you, And in you all the families of the earth shall be blessed."

JESUS DOES NOT WANT A BODY OF SOWERS
HE WANTS A BODY OF REAPERS

I trust the Lord to be with you and those you present the biblically strategized salvation gospel to and lead to their salvation in Jesus Christ. The body of Christ is called to "love the Lord and love people." The most loving thing a Christian can do for an unsaved person is to lead them to their decision for Christ. I know what you can accomplish with the biblically strategized salvation gospel presentation. You will be in His will, because you have learned to be a reaper, according to His word and you will be blessed in ways you have never imagined.

Acts 1:8 "But you shall receive power when the Holy Spirit has come upon you; and you shall be witnesses to Me in Jerusalem, and in all of Judea and Samaria, and to the end of the earth."

In this glorious statement He is telling the body of Christ that the Holy Spirit will be with us wherever we go. The body of Christ has been made in His image to do His will, which includes to go into all the world and be a reaper to make disciples. If you want to know where your mission field is located, it is not hard to find. Now that you know how to lead or win unsaved people to Christ, your mission field will be wherever you happen to be at the moment.

It is my honor and privilege to offer you this training on how to win souls in personal evangelism and I pray for your evangelism success. I look forward to a glorious day in heaven when I can meet you and also all those we've led to Christ, so we can all rejoice together. May God bless you, your family, God's plan for your life and all those you lead to Christ.

To order additional books as gifts or to encourage friends to order WHAT TO SAY EVANGELISM for themselves: go to westbowpress.com then click: Bookstore, look for the search menu and then type in the book title, WHAT TO SAY EVANGELISM

Thank You and May God Bless You, Your Family and Your Personal Evangelism Ministry,
Brent

Printed in the United States
by Baker & Taylor Publisher Services